Elite · 121

Ancient Siege Warfare

Persians, Greeks, Carthaginians
and Romans 546–146 BC

Duncan B Campbell · Illustrated by Adam Hook

First published in Great Britain in 2004 by Osprey Publishing
Elms Court, Chapel Way, Botley, Oxford OX2 9LP, United Kingdom
Email: **info@ospreypublishing.com**

CIP data for this publication is available from the British Library

ISBN 1 84176 770 0

Editor: Ruth Sheppard
Design: Alan Hamp
Index by Glyn Sutcliffe
Originated by The Electronic Page Company, Cwmbran, UK
Printed in China through World Print Ltd.

05 06 07 08 09   10 9 8 7 6 5 4 3 2 1

FOR A CATALOGUE OF ALL BOOKS PUBLISHED BY
OSPREY MILITARY AND AVIATION PLEASE CONTACT:

The Marketing Manager, Osprey Direct UKPO Box 140,
Wellingborough, Northants, NN8 2FA, United Kingdom
Email: info@ospreydirect.co.uk

Osprey Direct, 2427 Bond Street, University Park,
IL 60466, USA
Email: info@ospreydirectusa.com

By online at **www.ospreypublishing.com**

Dedication

For Janet, who has often wondered what her absent husband does
all day in the library; and for Ruairi, a most excellent young man.

Acknowledgements

I am pleased to acknowledge the generosity of colleagues who
supplied information and provided illustrations for this book:
Crawford H. Greenewalt, Jr., Thomas R. Martin, Franz Georg Maier,
Andreas L. Konecny, Nicholas D. Cahill, B. S. J. Isserlin, Donal
Bateson, Poul Pederson, Jodi Magness and Tamara Winikoff.
Once again, Mel Richmond worked her digital magic on my slides.

Author's Note

All ancient sources are referenced using the abbreviations
recommended by *The Oxford Classical Dictionary*. All translations
are my own.

Editor's Note

All attempts to trace and acknowledge the copyright holder of the
photograph on p.48 were ultimately unsuccessful. The publishers
would be happy to rectify any omissions if contacted.

ANCIENT SIEGE WARFARE
PERSIANS, GREEKS, CARTHAGINIANS AND ROMANS 546–146 BC

INTRODUCTION

THE HISTORY OF SIEGE WARFARE stretches back into the 2nd millennium BC. By that time, the towns of Mesopotamia (the land between the rivers Tigris and Euphrates in present-day Iraq) had become naturally defensive, sitting on the raised base (or 'tell') formed by earlier generations of mud-brick collapse. Tells, often 10 or 20m high, were crowned by town walls, and might be additionally defended by an encircling ditch further down the slope. Crenellations afforded protection to archers on the wall-walk, and towers allowed for long-range surveillance, as well as providing an elevated shooting platform.

Of course, as soon as people began to build walls around their possessions, others began to devise the means of appropriating these possessions. Equally, as a succession of Sumerian, Babylonian and Assyrian empires conquered their neighbours, new territory could only

View of Gaza taken in 1922. The mound on which the village sits represents centuries of occupation dating back to the 2nd millennium BC. It may have been this site that Alexander besieged in 322 BC.
(© École biblique, Jerusalem)

Assyrian siege warfare. A series of reliefs from Sennacherib's palace at Nineveh depict the siege of Lachish (Israel) in 701 BC. Here, the Assyrians advance their war machines up specially built ramps, and are met with a hail of burning torches from the battlements. (A. H. Layard, *Monuments of Nineveh*, London 1853)

be held by controlling the main towns. Thus, it was inevitable that sieges would play a central role in the conflicts that raged throughout the Near East in the 1st millennium BC. The siege tactics originally devised by the warlike Assyrians echoed down through the ages, and found employment wherever there was a need to capture strongholds.

The fundamentals of siege warfare

Towns did frequently surrender in terror at the approach of their enemy, but more often, the townsfolk barred the gates and hoped that their fortifications would discourage the aggressor. Under these circumstances, five courses of action remained open to the besieger. He could gain entry by crossing over the defences, penetrating through them, or tunnelling under them. If he failed in these, or perhaps lacked the means to attempt them, he might threaten the townsfolk with starvation by blockading their supply routes. The only remaining option was to gain access by treachery or trickery.

The most straightforward route over the defences involved ladders, but this was also the most perilous approach: the apparatus gave no protection, and the climbing individuals were vulnerable to attack from above. The alternative was to pile up an earth embankment high enough to overtop the walls, so that troops could storm up and over. But the construction of these massive ramps was labour intensive, and the process became increasingly risky as the workers drew nearer to the walls.

Breaking through the defences required battering rams, directed either at the wall itself or at a gateway. In theory, the latter represented the weakest point in a defensive circuit, and might even be vulnerable to fire; but for that reason any right-minded defender concentrated his efforts there. Alternatively, walls might be made to collapse by digging away their foundations or undermining long stretches, but both methods carried their own dangers. The third approach, passing beneath the defences, required the excavation of tunnels large enough

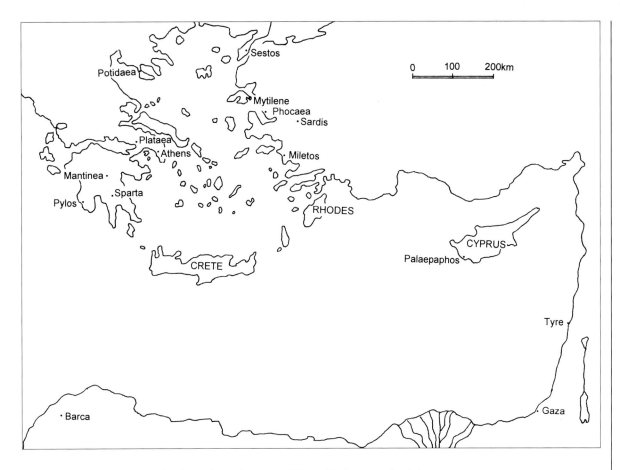

to deliver an effective strike force into the town. If handled properly, this method had the advantage of secrecy, but this would be lost as soon as the defenders either heard the tunnellers or noticed the accumulation of spoil from the excavation.

Sites in the eastern Mediterranean mentioned in the text. (© Author)

These methods, singly or in combination, offered the besieger a chance to rapidly seize a fortified town. However, he might suffer heavy casualties in the process. Far less dangerous from the besieger's perspective was the blockade: in theory, by sealing off the townsfolk from the outside world, privation would force them to surrender. However, depending upon the resources of the town and the totality of the blockade, such an operation might drag on indefinitely. This could be as disadvantageous to the besieger as to the besieged, because an army encamped in one location for a protracted period brought its own problems of supply and sanitation.

Of course, if political rivalry existed within the town, one or other faction might be persuaded to grant the besieger access, thus saving time and avoiding unnecessary losses. The besieger's only other option was to trick his way in. The standard form of trickery involved the conspicuous departure of the besieging forces, in apparent abandonment of the operation. The relieved townsfolk could then be caught off guard by a strike force that had been left behind in concealment; ideally, the latter's infiltration of the unsuspecting town was timed to coincide with the return of the main besieging force. The legendary capture of Troy was accomplished by just such a ruse.

The acropolis at Sardis, looking west across the ancient site towards the sanctuary of Artemis. The site of the Lydian city's west gate lies off to the right of the photo, and is obscured by the acropolis. (© Crawford H. Greenewalt, Jr.)

SIEGE WARFARE OF THE ACHAEMENID PERSIANS

Assyrian dominance had passed back to the Babylonians by around 600 BC. They, in turn, were eclipsed by the rise of the Achaemenid dynasty of Persians, with the accession of Cyrus the Great around 560 BC. His son Cambyses (r. 530–522 BC) was succeeded by Darius (r. 522–486 BC), whose designs on Greece were famously thwarted at Marathon in 490 BC. A second invasion of Greece, launched ten years later by Darius' son and successor Xerxes (r. 486–465 BC), similarly failed when the Persians were defeated at Plataea in 479 BC. The armies fielded by these Achaemenid kings seem to have been just as vigorous in siegecraft as their Assyrian forebears. The historical sources carry reports of siege equipment, undermining operations, and the construction of earth embankments to dominate town walls; trickery was also employed on occasion.

The conquests of Cyrus the Great

The Greek writer Xenophon took an interest in Persian affairs following his military service as a mercenary in the region in 401 BC. According to him, in 546 BC, when Cyrus annexed Lydia, the kingdom of Croesus in present-day Turkey, he ordered the construction of battering rams for an assault on the fabulously rich capital city of Sardis (Xen., *Cyr.* 7.2.2). However, after two weeks of fruitless siege, Cyrus offered to reward the first man to scale the walls. Many tried without success, until a

The 6th-century BC fortifications of Sardis at the west gate, viewed from the exterior. The intermittent glacis appears to have been an integral part of the defences, but the large rectilinear recess defies explanation. (Reconstruction drawing by Philip T. Stinson; © Archaeological Exploration of Sardis/Harvard University)

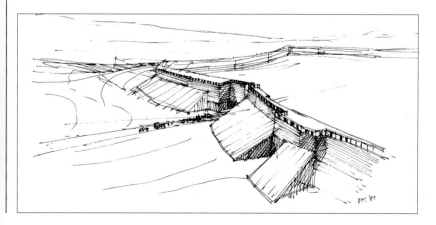

certain Hyroeades led the way up the steep slope to an unguarded section of the acropolis. The Greek historian Herodotus, who composed his *History* around 430 BC, tells the story. According to him, Hyroeades had observed one of Croesus' soldiers climbing down the cliff to retrieve his fallen helmet; he duly led a party of Persians up the same route, and the city was taken (Hdt. 1.84–86). The Roman writer Polyaenus, who published a collection of stratagems (*Stratēgēmata*) around AD 160, claimed that Cyrus had taken the town by trickery, feigning retreat before mounting a nocturnal escalade (*Strat.* 7.6.2); furthermore, he recorded that the Lydians sheltering on the acropolis were moved to surrender when Cyrus threatened to kill their captured relatives (*Strat.* 7.6.3). Although Polyaenus is an erratic source whose testimony should not be allowed to contradict a reliable authority like Herodotus, the latter mentions only the capture of the acropolis; it may be that, prior to this, the main fortification was taken by a ruse.

Western defences of Sardis, viewed from the interior of the town. The mud-brick wall sits on a low stonework plinth, and was preserved when the superstructure collapsed. It is now thought that the walls might have been as high as 30m. (© Archaeological Exploration of Sardis/Harvard University)

Herodotus and Xenophon both suggest that Cyrus was troubled by the choice between satisfying his men with plunder, and saving Sardis from destruction. When Croesus was captured during the siege, he asked Cyrus what the Persians were doing, to which the king allegedly replied, 'sacking your city and carrying off your property'; but Croesus retorted, 'it is *your* property they are plundering'. According to Herodotus, Croesus then advised Cyrus not to allow indiscriminate looting, but to gather all the booty on the pretext that one tenth had to be dedicated to the gods; Xenophon tells a similar tale. Whether true or not, it neatly highlights a problem that every siege commander eventually had to face.

During excavations at the site, the Harvard-led archaeological exploration of Sardis unearthed a 170m length of the Lydian town's mud-brick walls. The massive 20m-thick barrier, buttressed in front by a sloping earthwork glacis and still standing 15m high at some points, exhibits several peculiarities of design. For example, the stone 'socle', or plinth upon which the mud-brick walls were built, varies in height from around a metre up to 4.5m. In places, there was evidence that the wall had been violently destroyed, though whether during an assault or in the subsequent sack of the city remains unclear; perhaps the Persians adopted the standard Assyrian practice of slighting the walls of their defeated enemies. The forward tumble of mud-bricks showed signs of burning, and the debris sealed a 10cm-thick layer of burnt timber. Amid this dramatic evidence of destruction lay the skeleton of a young warrior, apparently poised to throw a stone. Aged in his mid-20s, he may have been a slinger or stone-thrower defending the walls to the last. An unusually ornate helmet found in fragments nearby need not have been his; however, medical autopsy showed that he had already sustained head wounds some years prior to death, which may have persuaded him to invest in a helmet.

The skeleton of a young man, discovered in 1987/8, amid the 6th-century debris in front of the town wall of Sardis. An apricot-sized stone is clasped in his right hand. Skeletal development, along with the nature of several previous injuries, suggested to the excavators that the man was a warrior. He had been stabbed in the middle of the back, but whether he had fallen, or his corpse had been dumped, is unknown. Another skeleton was later found in a nearby destruction layer.
(© Archaeological Exploration of Sardis/Harvard University)

The Persians in Ionia

Following his annexation of Lydia, Cyrus turned his attention to the Ionian Greek towns along the coast of Turkey, and entrusted their conquest to his generals. First, Mazares plundered Priene and Miletus, then Harpagus extended the operations to the remaining Greek communities; Herodotus explains that 'he enclosed them in their towns, and by piling up embankments against the walls he captured them' (Hdt. 1.162). Xenophon claims that Cyrus had prepared machinery and rams to batter the walls of anyone who refused to acknowledge his supremacy (*Cyr.* 7.4.1). But Herodotus mentions no siege equipment, and it is possible that the embankments were simply designed to elevate foot soldiers to rampart level, so that they could storm into the town.

At Phocaea in Turkey, Harpagus promised to restrain his troops, provided the townsfolk tore down one of their towers. But, taking advantage of their temporary reprieve, the Phocaeans evacuated their coastal town by sea, carrying off much of their property as well (Hdt. 1.164). Here, in the 1990s, archaeology brought to light a massively built wall, surviving to a height of around 5m where it had been preserved within a later tumulus, or burial mound. The wall was externally buttressed by a 3m-high stone-built glacis, perhaps to stabilise it against undermining. An attack had evidently been launched at the south gate, where there were signs of a conflagration: on the floor of the entrance lay carbonised fragments of the wooden uprights that once flanked the gate passage, and the excavator Ömer Özyiğit believed that a smashed amphora found there had been used to extinguish the fire. Certainly, the entrance way, originally of beaten earth, had been turned to mud, and in the process preserved two boot prints. Signs of conflict included Persian arrowheads littering the area and a single 22kg stone, which had probably been tumbled onto the attackers from the battlements above.

Cyrus' subsequent activities included the capture of Babylon, near present-day Baghdad (Iraq), in 539 BC. The Babylonian text known as the Nabonidus Chronicle claims that Babylon surrendered after Cyrus' brutal destruction of nearby Opis. Similarly, the Persian inscription known as the Cyrus Cylinder tells how the Babylonian god Marduk allowed Cyrus to capture the city peacefully: 'without battle or fighting, Marduk let him enter Babylon'. But Herodotus has a different story. According to him, the Persians lowered the level of the River Euphrates so that they could wade along it where it entered the city; the inhabitants were celebrating a local festival and had no warning of the Persian

infiltration until it was too late (Hdt. 1.191). Polyaenus preserves a similar version, perhaps taken from Herodotus (*Strat.* 7.6.5), but in a later passage he claims that the Persians drew off the Euphrates to deny drinking water to the townsfolk (*Strat.* 7.6.8). The story is a good one, but scholars are in general agreement that it must be an invention. It is possible that the Persians engineered the lowering of the river so as to be fordable by the army, but it is just as likely that the ancient writers were confused by a later irrigation project to connect the Tigris and Euphrates.

Darius and the Ionian Revolt

Soon after Darius came to power in 522 BC, Babylon again revolted. But having besieged the town for 19 months, the Persians could make no headway until a certain Zopyrus hatched a desperate scheme. First, he mutilated his own face to convince the Babylonians that he had fallen from Darius' favour; then, by staging a couple of victories over Persian troops, he gained the Babylonians' trust and admiration; and finally, having tricked his way into becoming guardian of Babylon, he threw open the gates to Darius (Hdt. 3.151–9).

Some years later, the Persian governor of Egypt launched an attack on the town of Barca in Libya. Over the course of nine months, the Persians attempted to tunnel into the town, but a Barcan metalworker devised an effective counter-measure. By placing the bronze facing of a shield on the ground at various points around the town circuit, he could detect where the Persians were tunnelling because the underground vibrations caused the bronze to resonate; countermines could then be dug to intercept the enemy (Hdt. 4.200). The stratagem became so well known that it was included in a compendium of advice for besieged towns, written almost 200 years later (Aeneas Tact. 37.6–7). In the end, unable to take the town by military assault, the Persian commander, Amasis, resorted to trickery. He invited a Barcan delegation to meet him in no man's land to make a pact. The Barcans agreed to pay tribute to

the Persians, and in return Amasis swore that he would never do them harm, for as long as the earth beneath their feet remained firm. However, unknown to the Barcans, they were standing, not on solid ground, but above a concealed trench that the Persians had dug during the previous night. The oath was thus void, and when the unsuspecting Barcans opened their gates the Persians seized the town. The townsfolk were enslaved and sent to Persia.

Of course, siege operations were not always successful. In 499 BC, the prosperous island of Naxos revolted against Persian rule, but the subsequent siege was abandoned after four months owing to the islanders' plentiful provisions (Hdt. 5.34). As a result of the Naxians' success, Aristagoras, the disaffected ruler of Miletus, roused other Greek towns along the coast of Asia Minor to join the so-called Ionian Revolt, which rumbled on for six years. He requested aid from mainland Greece, but only Athens and Eretria responded, contributing contingents to the army which sacked Sardis in 498 BC (Hdt. 5.99–102).

In the same year, the revolt spread to Cyprus, where a Persian army defeated the combined Cypriote forces in a pitched battle, and besieged the island's towns one by one. Soloi was the last to fall, when its walls were undermined in a five-month operation (Hdt. 5.115). At the town of Palaepaphos (modern Kouklia), archaeological work in the 1950s identified a large siege embankment near the north-east gate, filling the 3.7m defensive ditch and rising at least another 2.5m against the town wall. In a later remodelling of the defences, long after the siege, the embankment was landscaped into a projecting bastion encompassed by a retaining wall. It must originally have been longer, wider and higher than the surviving mound, but none of its original dimensions can be proven.

The Persian siege embankment at Palaepaphos during excavation. The town ditch can be seen to the right, while the town wall lies off the photo to the left. The two figures are standing above one of the tunnels dug by the defenders (Tunnel 1). Behind them can be seen the remains of the so-called sap, with vestiges of the mud-brick pillars and fire cauldron. (© F. G. Maier)

The attacking Persians used all available materials for its construction (see Plate A). In addition to earth, field stones, and tree trunks, there were more than 1,000 architectural and sculptural fragments; these pieces, which included statues, sphinxes, lions and altars, are thought to have come from a religious precinct, demolished by the Persians. Some 500 arrowheads and spear points, and over 400 roughly chiselled stone missiles, show that the construction work came under heavy fire from defenders on the town wall. In addition, traces of burnt bone among the embankment material, and the finds of a bronze helmet and fragments of an iron one, give an indication that desperate fighting must have occurred.

The excavations also revealed extensive remains of elaborate counter-siege operations. Using skills gained in local copper mining, the townsfolk attempted to destabilise the Persian embankment by driving a series of large tunnels underneath. In total, five tunnels were dug, one of which was technically a sap; this 1.5m-deep trench breached the town wall at its base and ran out for a further 12m, where it met the edge of the town's defensive ditch. Wooden props along both sides of the 2m wide passage must have supported a planked roof, and towards the end of the sap the roof gained additional support from three squat piers of mud-brick, arranged in a row along the centre. The other tunnels began immediately inside the town wall, dropping in roughly cut steps to a depth of about 2.4m to get beneath the wall's foundations, and running for a distance of about 20m to reach the town ditch. Emerging from the bedrock into the debris-filled ditch, the tunnellers no doubt boarded the walls and roof with timber. The width of each tunnel varied from 1.1m to 1.7m, and the headroom from 1.7m to 2.3m; niches were cut into the walls to hold clay lamps for illumination. The excavated rock was dragged back into the town and dumped at each tunnel mouth, along with material from the Persian embankment.

At the ends of Tunnels 1 and 3, and the sap, archaeologists found the remains of a large bronze cauldron, fire-damaged and filled with

Over 150 bronze spear and arrowheads were recovered from the embankment at Palaepaphos. Most of the arrowheads were triple-barbed and socketed; missiles of similar design are associated with other Persian find-spots, but the form may have been common throughout the Near East. (© F. G. Maier)

RIGHT The remains of mud-brick pillars and a disfigured bronze cauldron at the end of Tunnel 1 at Palaepaphos. (© F. G. Maier)

Bronze cauldrons were used to fire the timber props at the end of each Cypriote tunnel. This one is depicted *in situ* in the sap. Above each cauldron, the extreme heat had calcined the embankment material into a cone-shaped mass of lime. (© F. G. Maier)

carbonised wood and ash. Above each cauldron, the intense heat had fused the embankment material into a large cone of lime. It seems that, rather than steadily extracting the embankment material through the tunnels (as was later attempted at Plataea in 429 BC), the townsfolk hoped to cause sudden and unexpected slumping at the head of each mine by firing its wooden roof and causing internal collapse. The excavator, Franz Georg Maier, reasoned that this kind of localised destabilising meant that the targets were Persian siege towers on the embankment, but perhaps the Cypriotes had hoped that the conflagration would spread to the tree trunks and brushwood within the mound, causing wholesale destruction.

The easternmost tunnel, Tunnel 2, remained unfinished after about 15m, apparently owing to a roof collapse. Tunnels 1 and 3 headed directly north-east beneath the wall curtain and out to the town ditch. But the western tunnel, Tunnel 4, took a winding course under the town gateway, finally linking up with a lateral spur from Tunnel 3. Investigation showed that, at some point, the access to Tunnel 3 was completely blocked where it passed beneath the town wall. Consequently, it has been suggested that Tunnel 4 was dug in order to rescue miners trapped deep in Tunnel 3; certainly, the spur (designated Tunnel 3A) had headroom of only 0.6m for long stretches, perhaps implying that it was an emergency measure. Nevertheless, there is no certainty that Tunnel 3 was blocked during the siege, and an alternative explanation may be advanced for the reduced dimensions of 3A. This may have been designed to control the draught to the fire-chamber at the end of Tunnel 3, making it a more sophisticated version of Tunnel 1.

Unfortunately, the mines seem not to have had the desired effect. None of the fire-chambers was large enough to create major subsidence in the embankment, and the Persians must eventually have broken into the town, if not over the walls then certainly through the gateway, where excavation uncovered burnt debris containing arrowheads, javelin points and stone missiles. Herodotus records that 'the Cypriotes, after a year of freedom, were reduced once more to slavery' (Hdt. 5.116). There were still towns on the mainland to be subdued, and the Ionian Revolt

ended only with the fall of Miletus in 494 BC to Persian tunnelling; the town was plundered and the people carted off to the Persian capital at Susa (Hdt. 6.6, 18).

Persian siege machines

Little is known of the kind of siege apparatus employed by the Persians. Unlike their Assyrian forebears, the Achaemenids did not surround themselves with sculptural depictions of war, and none of their literary sources describes a siege. By contrast, in his idealised 'Education of Cyrus' (*Cyropaedia*), Xenophon represents the Great King ordering the manufacture of machinery (*Cyr.* 6.1.20–2), which he placed in the care of an engineering corps (*Cyr.* 6.3.8). However, we are not sure what these machines looked like. Xenophon's references to 'machines and ladders' (*Cyr.* 7.2.2) and 'machines and battering rams' (*Cyr.* 7.4.1) are too vague to help matters, but the French scholar Yvon Garlan assumed that they must be siege towers of some description. Cyrus certainly appears to have had such devices. Xenophon (*Cyr.* 6.1.52–54) describes one whose 'lowest storey including the wheels' stood about three *orguiai* (18 Greek feet, or 5.6m) high. It was crewed by 20 men, and the total weight of 120 talents (a little over 3 tonnes) was easily drawn by eight yoke of oxen. However, although such machines apparently accompanied each division of Cyrus' army, they seem not to have been intended for sieges, but to support the army on the battlefield.

Tunnel 4 at Palaepaphos has headroom of 1.4–1.8m and a width of 1.1–1.5m; the scale at the entrance is 0.5m.
(© F. G. Maier)

Periodically, scholars have suggested that the Persians must have had some form of artillery. Early speculations were based on biblical evidence. In Ezekiel's prophesy concerning the siege of Jerusalem in around 580 BC, the Greek version of the text (the so-called Septuagint) mentions *belostaseis*, or 'artillery positions' (Ezek. 4.2; 21.22). However, the original Hebrew text actually has the word *karim*, meaning battering rams, so the reference to artillery seems to have been an error made by the ancient Greek translators. In a different passage of scripture, King Uzziah of Judah is said to have defended Jerusalem around 760 BC with machines for shooting missiles and great stones (2 Chr. 26.15), but this is likely to be an anachronism. The chronicler was writing around 300 BC, by which time catapults were becoming common in the Near East, and it is easy to see how he might have elaborated his description with details from his own day. None of this biblical evidence would encourage a departure from the traditional date of 399 BC for the development of artillery.[1]

More recently, supporters of an earlier date for the catapult's introduction have been encouraged by archaeological finds from two Persian siege sites. At Palaepaphos on Cyprus, 422 roughly rounded limestone blocks were found, varying in diameter from 12cm to 28cm and weighing from 2kg to 22kg; by far the majority weighed 4–6kg. These came

1 See New Vanguard 89: *Greek and Roman Artillery 399 BC–AD 363.*

The Oxford historian George Rawlinson, brother of the Assyriologist Sir Henry Rawlinson, believed that the tall uprights at the right-hand edge of this Assyrian relief from Nimrud represented stone-throwing machines, but this identification is unconvincing. (Drawing by A. H. Layard of a wall relief, originally from the NW Palace of Ashurnasirpal II. © The British Museum)

A selection of the stone missiles from Palaepaphos. It is often suggested that these represent ammunition for stone-throwing machines, but it appears to have been common practice for defenders to heave boulders from the battlements onto the attackers below. (© F. G. Maier)

exclusively from outside the town defences, in the layer of debris associated with the Persian siege, which initially led the excavator to suggest that they derived from Persian catapults (Maier 1974). This view was tentatively advanced in Elisabeth Erdmann's final report, although she admitted that equipping the Persians with a primitive form of catapult was not an ideal explanation, and the stones could equally well have been dropped from the battlements.

The discovery of a stone missile during excavations at Phocaea in the 1990s re-opened the debate. The lump of tufa, found on the threshold of the gateway, was roughly worked into a sphere, 29cm in diameter and weighing 22kg (Özyiğit 1994). The Achaemenid specialist, Pierre Briant, was convinced that the weight of the stone argued against its use as a hand-thrown weapon and proposed that the Persian besiegers had used catapults (Briant 1994). That the stone belonged to the besiegers, and not to the defenders, was assumed by both Briant and Özyiğit on the grounds that it had been hastily manufactured; Briant added the argument that, if the Phocaeans had owned catapults, we would surely have heard about it. Unfortunately, the only author who records catapults at this early date is Polyaenus, whose collected *Stratēgēmata* veer wildly between plausibility and fiction depending on the source of the particular stratagem. According to him, when Cambyses, the son of Cyrus the Great, besieged Pelusium (Egypt) in 525 BC, the Egyptian defenders used 'catapults for sharp missiles, stones and fire' (*Strat.* 7.9); the story is probably false.

Of course, the hasty workmanship of the Phocaean missile does not prove a Persian origin; it could just as easily signify the emergency preparations of the defenders. But, contrary to common assumptions, a stone ball need not imply catapults at all. Certainly, a distance throw with such a missile would be out of the question, but a 22kg stone could easily have been dropped from the battlements onto the attackers below. Such a heavy stone might be difficult to manoeuvre into position, but smoothing the edges to make a rough sphere would allow it to be rolled. It seems that the case for Persian artillery at such an early date is far from proven.

SIEGE WARFARE IN CLASSICAL GREECE

Classical Greek warfare was based on the punitive raid, designed to provoke the adversary into pitched battle; the accepted code of conduct obliged the two sides to meet in the ritualised clash of hoplite armies. Herodotus explains this in a speech that he puts into the mouth of the Persian Mardonius on the eve of Xerxes' invasion of Greece (Hdt. 7.9). By and large, there was no question of capturing towns or enslaving enemy populations. Of course, many Greeks would have been familiar with besieging techniques: their cousins in Asia Minor had seen Persian siegecraft at first hand during the Ionian Revolt, and Greek mercenaries had served with the Great King's army. But the resources of the average city-state would not have stretched to supporting the siege of a walled town.

Consequently, Greek armies lacked practice in this branch of warfare. This is illustrated by the Spartan attempt, around 525 BC, to overthrow the tyranny of Polycrates on the island of Samos. The Spartans initially gained a foothold on the town's seaward wall, perhaps by escalade, but were ejected from the town by overwhelming forces. In the mêlée, two of their number rushed through the open gates, but were killed inside the town. The Spartans had reached the limit of their besieging skills and departed after 40 days (Hdt. 3.54–6). An event in 489 BC shows that contemporary Athenian siegecraft was just as rudimentary. In the aftermath of the Greek victory at Marathon, the Athenian general Miltiades tried to punish the island town of Paros for having aided the Persians. But, with the Parians safe within their walls, the only tactic available to the Athenians was to devastate the island, and after 26 days they gave up and left (Hdt. 6.133–5). The Spartan-led coalition outside Thebes in 479 BC found themselves in a similar predicament. The Persian invaders had just been defeated at nearby Plataea, ending their aspirations of Greek conquest, but Thebes was harbouring Persian sympa-

Scene from the François Vase, showing Hector emerging from one of the gates of Troy. The artist's inclusion of stones, piled at intervals along the battlements, shows that this was a standard defensive measure used by Greek towns. (© Author)

Relief sculpture from the Nereid Monument (Block 872). Three soldiers are depicted scaling an assault ladder, while crouching archers provide covering fire. Note that the hoplites appear to be climbing one-handed, in order to maintain a grip on their shields. (© The British Museum)

thisers. Fortunately for the Spartans, the traitors gave themselves up after only 20 days of siege (Hdt. 9.86–7).

Athenian siegecraft

At some point, the Athenians acquired a reputation for siegecraft. The historian Thucydides says as much (1.102), although as an Athenian and a soldier he is perhaps a biased source. It is true that, following the battle of Plataea in 479 BC, the Spartans were unable to break into the Persian stockade, where the survivors were rallying, until the Athenian forces arrived (Hdt. 9.70). But when the Roman biographer Plutarch came to retell the story, it seems as though the Spartans were simply inexperienced in storming walls (Plut., *Aristides* 19). A comparison may be drawn with an incident from the battle at Mycale, allegedly fought on the same day as Plataea; during the rout of the Persian forces by the allied Greeks, it was the Athenian contingent that led the assault on the enemy stockade (Hdt. 9.102). As Garlan rightly observed, the supposed Athenian expertise was tested only against wooden palisades, not real fortifications.

Another event from 479 BC points up this contrast. The Persian bridgehead on the European side of the Hellespont was based at Sestos, which remained in Persian hands even after Xerxes' withdrawal from Greece. This strongly fortified town was strategically placed to challenge Athenian trade with the Black Sea region, so Xanthippus, the father of Pericles, led an Athenian fleet to capture it. The Persian governor Artayctes was unprepared for siege, so starvation quickly set in. Yet, despite this fact, the Athenians made little headway and complained to their officers, requesting to be taken home. It was only with the escape of Artayctes that the townsfolk were free to open their gates to the Athenians (Hdt. 9.114–121; Diod. Sic. 11.37.4–5). Similarly, the blockade of Persian-garrisoned Eion by Cimon, the son of Miltiades, was only brought to a conclusion when the Persian general Butes set fire to the place, preferring to perish than to be starved into submission (Plut., *Cimon* 7); the method of capture is not recorded by Thucydides (1.98), but a note by the Hadrianic traveller and writer Pausanias suggests that Cimon had diverted the town's water supply (Paus. 8.8.9).

It is clear that the Athenians had developed no revolutionary besieging tactics. During the 470s and 460s BC, in the course of building their maritime empire under the guise of the Delian League, they often found it necessary to bring recalcitrant towns into line, but this was done not with an aggressive assault but by employing the costly method of blockade. Thasos provides a case in point. When the island revolted in around 465 BC, the ensuing Athenian siege dragged on into a third year before the Thasians surrendered; their walls were slighted, their navy was confiscated, and an annual tax was imposed (Thuc. 1.101). At Samos in 440 BC, Pericles is said to have erected blockading walls on three sides of the town (Thuc. 1.116), while Athenian ships patrolled the fourth side, which lay on the coast. When the ships briefly departed, the Samians took the opportunity to raid their oppressor's fleet base and bring in supplies; but, on the return of the Athenian ships, the blockade was once more complete, and the Samians finally capitulated after nine months (Thuc. 1.117).

Blockading walls

Athens dealt similarly with Potidaea, which refused the unreasonable Athenian demands to dismantle its fortifications late in 432 BC. Sited on the westernmost finger of Chalcidice at the narrowest point, its walls ran from sea to sea, dividing the southern peninsula from the land mass to the north. The Persians had failed to storm the town during their retreat from Greece in 479 BC, but this was largely down to the incompetence of their commander (Hdt. 8.126–9). The Athenians adopted a different tack: two blockading walls were constructed, one to the north of the town and one to the south, completely barring the isthmus, and naval patrols watched both coasts (Thuc. 1.64). Unfortunately, the town proved surprisingly stubborn; in the second year of the siege, fresh forces from Athens made a vain attempt to storm the place using 'machines' (a word which Thucydides often uses to mean ladders), but their failure was compounded by an outbreak of plague and, after 40 days, they withdrew again (Thuc. 2.58). By this time, the Potidaeans had reportedly been reduced to cannibalism, and finally surrendered after a siege of over two years (Thuc. 2.70; Diod. Sic. 12.46.2–6).

In Greek art, representations of sieges tend to be mythological rather than historical. This scene from an Etruscan ash urn is thought to depict the tale of the 'Seven against Thebes', which culminated in the assault on the town by a group of heroes. It is noteworthy that two of the three defenders are shown dropping large stones onto their adversaries. (© Author)

During the Peloponnesian War (431–404 BC), Athens used the technique of encirclement (*periteichismos*) several times, for example in 428 BC, when its erstwhile ally Mytilene on the island of Lesbos revolted. Here, the surrounding siege wall incorporated strongpoints for the Athenian garrison, but their blockade failed to prevent a Spartan agent from slipping into the town by way of a dry river bed. Fortunately for Athens, the Spartan plan to relieve Mytilene backfired when arms distributed among the townsfolk were used in a popular uprising. The

Potidaea from the north-west. The ancient town straddled the narrow isthmus and apparently could only be by-passed at low tide. No substantial remains can now be seen, owing to the presence of the modern town of Nea Potidaea and the cutting of a canal to link the Thermaic and Toronaic Gulfs.
(© Thomas R. Martin & Ivy S. Sun. Image courtesy of The Perseus Digital Library, http://www.perseus.tufts.edu)

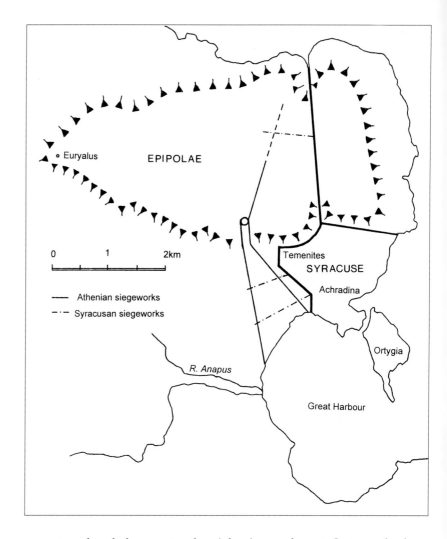

At Syracuse, the Athenian blockade ended in failure. Having established the 'circle' fort as a strongpoint on the Epipolae plateau, the Athenians secured their links to the harbour by driving twin siege walls southwards, breaking through successive Syracusan counter-works. However, the northward extension of the siege-works was delayed, and was finally thwarted by the Syracusans. (© Author)

town was handed over to the Athenians, who at first resolved to exterminate everyone, but were subsequently satisfied with the deaths of the 1,000 males who had taken part in the revolt (Thuc. 3.18, 25, 27–8, 36, 50). The Athenians were more ruthless at Melos, which they placed under siege in 416 BC for refusing to pay tribute. Different troop contingents vied with one another in building the encircling siege wall, and vigilance was increased after the townsfolk twice managed to bring in supplies through a weak sector. In the following year, when the town finally surrendered, all of the men were put to death, and the women and children were sold into slavery (Thuc. 5.114.1–2, 115.4, 116.2–3).

By that time, the *periteichismos* had become an Athenian hallmark. In 426 BC, the Acarnanian troops accompanying Demosthenes' Athenian army at Leucas urged him to surround the town with walls, in order to speed the townsfolk's surrender (Thuc. 3.94). Sieges occasionally took a different course, as at Mende, south of Potidaea, where internal squabbling between the townsfolk and the Peloponnesian garrison installed by Sparta gave the Athenians an ideal opportunity to burst into the town and subject it to wholesale plundering (423 BC); but the acropolis proved impregnable, so they resorted to constructing siege walls (Thuc. 4.130). Shortly afterwards, Mende's neighbour, Scione, was surrounded with Athenian siege-works; but before the encirclement was complete, troops from Mende managed to break out and slip into Scione (Thuc. 4.131, 133). It did them little good, for they finally succumbed two years later and were put to death; the women and children were enslaved and the land given over to Athenian allies (Thuc. 5.32). As late as 409 BC, the technique was still in favour when the Athenians forced the surrender of Chalcedon by surrounding the town with a palisade (Diod. Sic. 13.66.1–3; Xen., *Hell.* 1.3.4–7); a similar strategy failed at Byzantium, until the town was betrayed from within (Diod. Sic. 13.66.3–67.7; Xen., *Hell.* 1.3.14–22).

The Athenian attack on the little island of Minoa in 428 BC demonstrates that, occasionally, a more direct approach was tried. The city-state of Megara, on the adjacent coast, had built a fort there, but the Athenian general Nicias captured it by landing 'machines' from the sea (Thuc. 3.51). The classicist Eric Marsden, best known for his work on ancient artillery, thought that these machines might have been ship-mounted siege towers. He was perhaps thinking of the transport vessel that the Athenians equipped with wooden towers for fighting in the harbour at Syracuse (Thuc. 7.25), but this could never have been used for an amphibious assault. It seems more likely that Nicias' machines were simply assault ladders. The Athenians planned to use the island as a springboard for an attempt on the coastal town of Nisaea, which had been garrisoned by the Spartans' Peloponnesian allies, but the attack, when it came, took the form of the familiar blockade.

The Megarians had built a pair of 'long walls' linking their town to Nisaea, in order to safeguard the route to the harbour there. However, in 424 BC, 600 Athenian troops crossed by night from Minoa and managed to infiltrate these walls, severing Nisaea's link to Megara. Reinforced by 4,000 hoplites and gangs of stonemasons, they built a wall and ditch around the town, utilising materials salvaged from the suburbs and even incorporating entire buildings into their work; in two days, the *periteichismos* was complete and the Peloponnesian garrison surrendered (Thuc. 4.66–69).

Only at Syracuse did the Athenian strategy of *periteichismos* prove disastrous (see Plate B), but this can largely be blamed on poor leadership. In 415 BC, when Athens decided to extend its influence to Sicily by capturing this prosperous port city, an entire year was squandered in minor skirmishing, giving the Syracusans time to organise their defence and enlist Spartan assistance. Early in 414 BC, the Athenians took control of the Epipolae plateau overlooking the city, and built a fort at Syca as the pivotal point of the inevitable siege wall. By midsummer, a double wall extended south from the plateau to the harbour, despite Syracusan attempts to intercept it with palisades (Thuc. 6.97–101), but the Athenians delayed completion of the siege-works to the north. This fundamental blunder was quickly exploited by the Syracusans, under the leadership of the newly arrived Spartan general Gylippus. They intercepted the line of the siege wall with their own cross wall, which, adding insult to injury, was built with the stones already laid out for the Athenian wall (Thuc. 7.4–6). With one action, they had turned the tables on the Athenians, thwarting their blockade of the city.

The Oxford scholar G. B. Grundy memorably summed up the Athenians' fame in siegecraft as 'the reputation of the one-eyed among the blind'. But if their reputation was not based on conspicuous success, it perhaps arose from their ability to organise and finance the labour required to prosecute such an operation. Certainly, of the allied army besieging Miletus in 411 BC, it was the Athenian contingent that contemplated building siege walls (Thuc. 8.25). Of course, a blockade could be maintained without siege-works, but the Athenian predilection for constructing them suggests that real benefits were perceived. Quite apart from the protection of the besieging forces, and the concealment of their movements from the besieged, there were perhaps psychological factors involved, for the visual impact of a siege wall sent the message to the defenders that their plight was hopeless.

Spartan siegecraft

The Spartans' incapacity for siegecraft has become notorious, but is easily explained by the practicalities of hoplite warfare. The Spartans had dominated the Peloponnese by their success on the battlefield. When their army threatened the farmland of neighbouring city-states, the inhabitants could not afford the luxury of remaining behind their walls, allowing their annual produce to be ravaged; economic necessity forced them to take the field, and this was where the Spartan army excelled. Consequently, where there was little need for siegecraft, there was no opportunity to learn.

The Spartan invasion of Acarnania in 429 BC demonstrates this. The unfortified village of Limnaea was easily sacked, but the walls of Stratus were a more daunting prospect; the Spartans seem to have had no other strategy than the hope that the overawed townsfolk would open their gates (Thuc. 2.80–1). Similarly, in an attack on Naupactus in 426 BC, the Spartans seized the unwalled sector of the town without any trouble, but when they saw that the walled sector was fully garrisoned they departed (Thuc. 3.102). Some years earlier, they had attempted to attack Oenoe 'using machines and other means' (Thuc. 2.18), but every attempt failed. So daunted by walls were they that, in their attack on Mantinea in 385 BC, the Spartans dammed the river Ophis, which flowed through the town, in order to raise the water level and dissolve the mud-brick walls (Paus. 8.8.7; Diod. Sic. 15.12.1–2; Xen., *Hell.* 5.2.4–6).

Such tactical limitations were not confined to Sparta. When the Thebans decided to attack their hated neighbour, Plataea, in 431 BC, it was treachery that gained them entry to the town; but the advance guard of 300 men failed to subjugate the townsfolk and ended up dead or captured (Thuc. 2.2–4). In 428 BC, the Mytilenians' attempt on neighbouring Methymna came to nothing when the hoped-for betrayal failed to materialise (Thuc. 3.18). Thucydides reports that the Argives, who failed to storm Epidaurus by escalade early in 418 BC, only made the attempt because they thought the place was undefended (Thuc. 5.56). Later the same year, a combined force of Mantineans and Eleans successfully cowed the town of Orchomenus by making repeated assaults on a weak fortification; fearing that the large allied army would eventually

At Pylos, the Athenians spent six days fortifying the headland, but with only one spring and no harbour the position was poor from a logistical standpoint. However, Sphacteria was even worse; the Spartans stranded there had to rely on swimmers to bring foodstuffs across. But it was only when the forest cover on the island was accidentally torched that the Spartan position became vulnerable. (© Author)

OPPOSITE **The 18th-century *Chevalier* de Folard's interpretation of the Spartan *periteichismos* at Plataea.** Thucydides describes two concentric walls, with a 16-foot (4.9m) space in between for the garrison; his observation, that the entire work looked like a single thick wall battlemented on either side, is usually taken to mean that the space was roofed over, as shown here. (Author's collection)

The site of Plataea, looking north from the slopes of Mount Cithaeron. The wall delimiting the acropolis plateau is probably late Roman, but may well follow the line of the Classical Greek wall. No remains of siege-works have been found.
(© Andreas L. Konecny)

break in, the town surrendered (Thuc. 5.61). Speedy capitulation was evidently preferable to resistance, which might aggravate resentment among the besieging forces and result in atrocities should the town fall.

The events at Pylos in 425 BC resulted in siegecraft of a sort. When Demosthenes fortified the headland as a thorn in Sparta's side, the ensuing combined land and sea assault by Spartan troops was badly mismanaged. By striking before the Athenian fleet arrived, they hoped to capture the place easily, 'because it was unprovisioned, since it had been seized in haste' (Thuc. 4.8). However, although on the landward side there was a stand-off with the Peloponnesian besiegers, on the seaward side Demosthenes' palisade frustrated the Spartan attacks there on two consecutive days. Meanwhile, as a fail-safe, the Spartans also landed 420 hoplites on the offshore island of Sphacteria, in case the Athenians planned to use it to dominate the bay around Pylos. But when the Athenian fleet finally arrived, the Spartan ships were put to flight, marooning their comrades on the island. And so, the Spartan siege of Pylos became an Athenian siege of Sphacteria, run

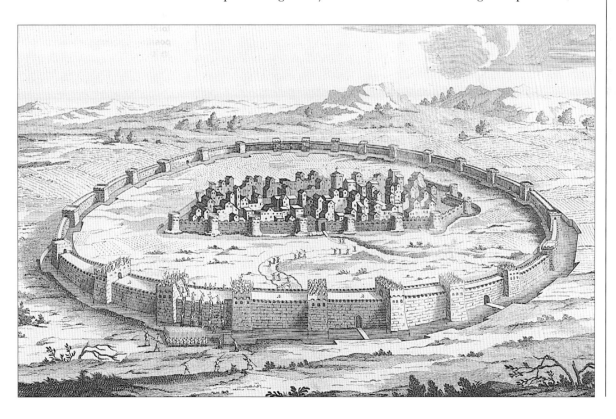

along the familiar lines of the blockade. It was only when it became apparent that the besieged Spartans were being provisioned by blockade-runners, that Demosthenes was obliged to take more active measures: landing a force of 800 hoplites, 800 archers and 2,000 light troops, he surrounded and overwhelmed the Spartans (Thuc. 4.31–9).

In view of this history of ineptitude, it is all the more surprising to find that the Spartans were responsible for the first reliably recorded Greek assault on a town wall using the scientific methods of the Persians. In 429 BC, the Spartan king Archidamus arrived before Plataea at the head of a Peloponnesian army, intent on avenging the slight suffered by his Theban allies two years earlier; the little town's allegiance to Athens was a further incentive for the attack. The standard request for the town's surrender was rejected, so Archidamus ordered the ravaging of the countryside, and the Peloponnesians planted a palisade all around the town 'to prevent any sorties' (Thuc. 2.75).

It is the next stage that has mystified scholars, for the Peloponnesians proceeded to raise a siege embankment against the town wall. Exactly why they decided upon this tactic is a mystery, but Archidamus is known to have been in contact with the Persians, and may have benefited from their advice on siegecraft. Timber was felled on nearby Mount Cithaeron and assembled into twin buttresses, arranged perpendicular to the town wall; between these, earth, stones and brushwood were piled up to create a giant ramp. In the meantime, the Plataeans did not stand idle, but raised the height of their town wall where it was threatened by the embankment, and erected screens of rawhide as a protection against fire. Then they secretly broke through their own wall where it abutted the embankment, and began extracting soil into the town; although their scheme was soon exposed and the gap stopped up, nevertheless the Plataeans persevered by tunnelling farther underneath the embankment. Simultaneously, they began the construction of a crescent-shaped wall as a second line of defence if the main wall should fail. At this point, the Peloponnesians brought up battering rams, but were frustrated by the defenders' counter-measures, which involved lassoing the ramming beams or snapping off their heads by dropping heavy timbers (Thuc. 2.75–6).

Having failed in their Persian-style attack, the Peloponnesians resorted to the tactic favoured by their Athenian enemies, namely *periteichismos*. They surrounded Plataea with a double wall of mud-brick, battlemented and provided with towers like a town wall; ditches ran around the inner and outer lines, where the material for the bricks had been extracted. The blockade dragged on for 18 months before the Plataeans finally mounted a desperate escape; on a dark and stormy night, 212 men used ladders to cross the wall unseen, and fled. The remaining 200 defenders held out six months longer before finally surrendering, whereupon the Spartans executed all of the males and enslaved the women (Thuc. 2.78; 3.20–24; 3.52; 3.68).

The technique of encirclement was not attempted by Spartan armies for another 40 years; but, having thrown a wall and ditch around Mantinea (385 BC), they decided upon other tactics (Xen., *Hell.* 5.2.4–6). Nor did the technique catch on with other city-states. Another 20 years passed before the Arcadians used a double palisade to encircle the Spartan-garrisoned town of Cromnus (365 BC); a relieving force failed to extricate the besieged, and they were subsequently distributed as prisoners among the Arcadian allies (Xen., *Hell.* 7.4.21–7).

Greek siege machines

Later writers occasionally claimed that the Greeks used siege machinery, but they were perhaps deceived by the exaggerated tradition of Athenian expertise. For example, at Paros in 489 BC, Miltiades clearly hoped to entice the defenders out from behind their walls, as he lacked the means of breaking into the town. However, when Cornelius Nepos came to write his *Life of Miltiades* in the 30s BC, he added 'shelters and sheds' (*vineis ac testudinibus*) of the sort employed by his Roman contemporaries when they were engaged in aggressive siegecraft (Nep., *Milt.* 7). Diodorus Siculus, writing around the same time as Nepos, claimed that it was actually during Pericles' siege of Samos, long after Miltiades had died, that the Greeks first used sheds and battering rams (Diod. Sic. 12.28.3). The story was repeated a century later by Plutarch, who said that he had got it from Ephorus (Plut., *Pericles* 27). But this historian's work, which survives only in fragments, was written fully 100 years after the siege of Samos, by which time siege machines were commonplace; in any case, Plutarch adds that not everyone believed the tale.

Amid the general catalogue of besieging incompetence, Pausanias' report of the siege of Oeniadae has understandably been doubted by scholars. According to him, the Messenians undermined the walls and brought up machinery (*mēchanēmata*) for battering down the fortifications (Paus. 4.25.2), whereupon the townsfolk withdrew under truce, to avoid the horrors of a storming assault. However, it is most likely that Pausanias added details familiar to him from Roman imperial siegecraft, but alien to the 5th century BC.

In general, Greek writers used the term 'machines' (*mēchanai*) to refer to a whole range of devices. Thucydides twice refers to the Spartan machines battering the walls at Plataea; from the context (and from Thucydides' use of the word *embolē*, which usually denotes the ram on a ship), these are clearly battering rams, though presumably of a fairly rudimentary design, given the ease with which the Plataeans neutralised them. On another two occasions, Thucydides uses the word 'machine' in reference to the crude but ingenious flame-throwers which enemy forces used against Athenian timber fortifications at Delium and Lecythus in 424 BC. And, in 403 BC, the Athenians so feared the arrival of 'machines' from Piraeus that, on the advice of a *mēchanopoios* ('engineer'), they unloaded boulders onto the road to hinder their progress (Xen., *Hell.* 2.4.27); unfortunately, we cannot say what kind of wheeled contraptions these were. Nevertheless, the remaining eight appearances of the word in Thucydides' *History* seem to refer to assault ladders, and there is no reason to suppose that anything more elaborate was used, under normal circumstances, by the Greeks.

Thucydides describes a flame-thrower used by the Boeotians at Delium. Two hollow wooden beams were joined to make a long pipe, and a good proportion was iron-plated. Bellows were inserted at the back end, and a cauldron was hung from chains at the front end. An iron tube, running along inside the pipe, projected from the front, where it curved down into the cauldron. The machine was manoeuvred into position on carts, and when the bellows were operated, the mixture of coal, sulphur and pitch in the cauldron produced a burst of flame. (© Author, after Warry)

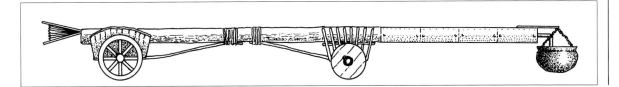

SIEGE WARFARE IN THE TIME OF DIONYSIUS I

In the years following the Peloponnesian War, western siege technology made a great leap forward on Sicily, when the Carthaginians of north Africa renewed their claim to the island. A previous attempt in 480 BC by General Hamilcar had been confounded by Gelon, whose kingdom centred around the city of Syracuse and represented the major power on the island. On that occasion, he inflicted a massive defeat on the Carthaginians, while they were occupied in blockading the town of Himera (Diod. Sic. 11.20–22).

For several generations afterwards, the Carthaginians remained disinclined to dabble in Sicilian affairs, although they maintained an interest in the north-west corner of the island, around the towns of Motya and Panormus. However, in 410 BC, the town of Segesta petitioned their aid against Selinus, an overbearing ally of Syracuse. The Carthaginian sovereign at that time was Hannibal, grandson of the Hamilcar who had died at Himera in 480 BC; according to the historian Diodorus, he was burning for revenge (Diod. Sic. 13.43.6).

Carthaginian sieges

Hannibal brought 'machinery for sieges, missiles, and all the other equipment' (Diod. Sic. 13.54.2), which he unleashed onto the unsuspecting Greek towns of Sicily in the style of his Persian forebears. First, at Selinus, he divided his forces into two, probably deployed on opposite sides of the town; then 'he set up six towers of excessive height, and thrust forward against the walls an equal number of iron-braced battering rams' (Diod. Sic. 13.54.7). His machinery towered over the defences, which had in any case fallen into disrepair, and his archers and slingers easily picked off the defenders as they manned the walls (Diod. Sic. 13.55.6–7). A similar strategy was followed at Himera, where 'he camped around the city' (Diod. Sic. 13.59.6) before setting his machines to shake the walls at several different locations. Although no siege towers were deployed, 'he also undermined the wall and put wood under as a support, and when this was set on fire a long section of the walls suddenly fell down' (Diod. Sic. 13.59.8); such chilling efficiency contrasts with Hamilcar's failed siege of the same town in 480 BC. At Akragas in 406 BC, Hannibal opened the attack with two enormous siege towers (Diod. Sic. 13.85.5), but when the defenders burned them

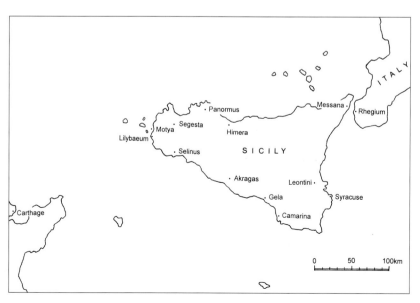

Broadly speaking, the towns in the eastern half of Sicily were Greek foundations, which exercised control over the native Sicel population; Carthage had colonised the western tip. Besides dominating affairs on Sicily, Syracuse extended its control into southern Italy. (© Author)

down, he resorted to piling up embankments in the Persian manner. His men demolished monuments and tombs outside the town to provide the building materials (Diod. Sic. 13.86.1), in a striking replay of events at Palaepaphos 90 years earlier. Finally, at Gela, Hannibal's successor, Himilcon, battered the walls with rams, but the townsfolk repeatedly repaired the breaches by night (Diod. Sic. 13.108.8), and the Carthaginians only managed to break in when the inhabitants finally fled the town.

Carthaginian warfare was characterised by its cruelty. It is not unlikely that the frustration of a protracted besieging assault was usually vented on the townsfolk. The Athenian playwright Aeschylus, who had famously fought at Marathon in 490 BC, lamented that 'many and wretched are the miseries when a city is taken' (Aesch., *Sept.* 339). It is true that Greek armies of the 5th century had been known to commit atrocities; the treatment of Plataea by the Spartans and of Melos by the Athenians are just two examples. However, Diodorus expresses particular revulsion for the behaviour of Hannibal's mercenaries as they sacked Selinus. Some of the townsfolk were burned alive in their homes, others were slaughtered defenceless in the streets, women were raped, and religious precincts violated (Diod. Sic. 13.57.2–5, 58.1–2; cf. 111.4).

Carthaginian siege machines

The Carthaginians traced their descent from Phoenicia, in particular the city of Tyre, and they seem to have followed the Persian tradition of siege warfare. The Roman architect-engineer Vitruvius, and his contemporary, the Greek Athenaeus, both attributed the invention of the battering ram to the Carthaginians. The story goes that, while besieging Gades possibly around 500 BC, the Carthaginians were unable to demolish the town walls, until they realised that a wooden beam could be used to gradually batter the wall from the top downwards, course by course. Similarly, the same two writers credited Pephrasmenos of Tyre with being the first to suspend the ramming beam from a frame, rather than having men carry it, while the distinction of raising the whole machine on wheels was granted to a Carthaginian named Geras (Vitr., *De arch.* 10.13.1–2; Ath., *Mech.* 3 [9.4–10.4]).

Another Roman writer, the elder Pliny, thought that the *ballista* and the sling were Phoenician inventions (Pliny, *HN* 7.201), and even though the attribution is almost certainly wrong it was obviously considered plausible by the ancients. Similarly, the Carthaginians cannot have been the inventors of battering technology, as the Assyrians were already using mobile rams around 850 BC; nevertheless, these stories demonstrate that they were perceived as a besieging nation.

Dionysius I of Syracuse

Carthaginian successes against the towns of Sicily alarmed Dionysius, the Greek tyrant of Syracuse (r. 406–367 BC). While extending his control over eastern Sicily, he experienced an initial setback at Leontini because he lacked siege machinery (Diod. Sic. 14.14.3–4); the inhabitants were soon cowed by the sight of their neighbours falling under Syracusan influence, but the experience must have taught Dionysius a lesson. As well as strengthening his city's fortifications, which now encompassed the exposed Epipolae plateau, he assembled craftsmen from all over the Mediterranean world to equip his arsenal; attracted by the promise of high wages, men came from Italy, Greece and even Carthage. All kinds of armaments were manufactured, including catapults, which Diodorus says were invented at that time (Diod. Sic. 14.42.1; cf. 50.4), and 'unfamiliar machinery that was capable of offering great advantages' (Diod. Sic. 14.42.2). Long afterwards, it was remembered that 'the whole area of machine construction developed under Dionysius the tyrant of the Sicilians' (Ath., *Mech.* 4 [10.5–7]).

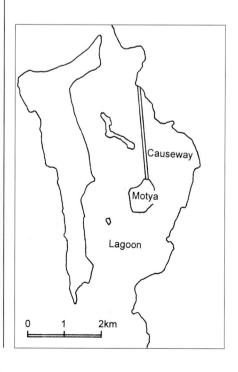

The island of Motya is situated in a lagoon. The remains of an artificial causeway, by which it was linked to the Sicilian mainland in antiquity, are still visible beneath the water. (© Author)

Having declared war on Carthage, Dionysius marched west, launching assaults on Panormus, Segesta and Entella; but the main focus was the offshore town of Motya, a colony of Carthage and its main supply base on Sicily (see Plate C). As a defensive measure, the townsfolk had severed the artificial causeway linking the island town to the shore, so Dionysius' first task was to repair it for the advance of his heavy machinery (Diod. Sic. 14.48.2; 49.3). When the Carthaginian navy attempted to intervene, they were repulsed by shipborne missile troops and by 'catapults for sharp missiles' lining the shore (Diod. Sic. 14.50.1–4). Scholars have debated whether Dionysius already possessed torsion catapults of the sort used by Alexander the Great and his successors. But it seems more likely that he relied upon the *gastraphetēs* and its larger cousins, which drew their power from over-sized composite bows; such weapons were unfamiliar at the time, and would easily have taken the Carthaginians by surprise.[2]

Diodorus' reference to 'machines of every kind' advancing along the causeway at Motya is characteristic hyperbole. (He also frequently refers to 'missiles of every kind'.) Besides the catapults, only battering rams and six-storey wheeled towers are specifically mentioned. Machines were also used at Caulonia in 389 BC (Diod. Sic. 14.103.3); and for his siege of Rhegium in the following year, Dionysius 'prepared a great quantity of machinery of incredible size, with which he shook the walls, striving to capture the town by force' (Diod. Sic.

2 See New Vanguard 89: *Greek and Roman Artillery 399 BC–AD 363*, plate A.

14.108.3). At Motya, the townsfolk countered Dionysius' assault with the age-old defence of fire. The Syracusans evidently had not yet devised an effective means of fire-proofing, for they were obliged to quench the flames wherever they caught hold (Diod. Sic. 14.51.1–3); perhaps teams of water carriers were detailed to pass buckets hand-to-hand from the surrounding lagoon.

Once the Syracusans had broken into Motya, the design of their siege towers allowed drawbridges to be lowered onto the house roofs, and prolonged hand-to-hand fighting ensued, until the attackers prevailed by sheer weight of numbers. In the chaos, only those who had taken refuge in the temples were spared, and the town was plundered. It was a different story at Rhegium, which held out for almost a year before starvation forced its surrender; the 6,000 who survived were sent to Syracuse as slaves (Diod. Sic. 14.111.1–4).

However, siege machinery was not the universal key to capturing fortified towns. As Dionysius realised at Motya, heavy machines required a smooth, flat running surface, but even then they did not guarantee rapid success, as the case of Rhegium shows. In an earlier attempt on the town, in 393 BC, Dionysius sprang a nocturnal escalade, no doubt hoping to

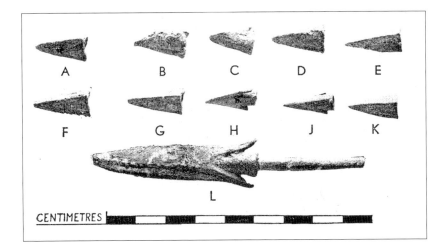

CENTIMETRES

Many arrowheads found at Motya are of a pyramidal, socketed type, commonly found on Sicily (here, A–G, K). This form, and its barbed variant (H, J), also have a wider Greek distribution, as do the larger, tanged arrowheads (L). Marsden suggested that some of these might have been used by Dionysius' *gastraphetai*. (Reprinted with the permission of B. S. J. Isserlin)

avoid the toil of bringing up machinery; part of his strategy was to burn the gates down, but the townsfolk deliberately fed the conflagration, so that the flames prevented the Syracusans from entering (Diod. Sic. 14.90.5–6). On other occasions, machinery simply could not be deployed. The mountain town of Tauromenium, for example, was scarcely accessible to infantry, far less wheeled machines. In 394 BC, when Dionysius launched a daring mid-winter assault on the rocky snow-clad citadel, his men were wrong-footed by the defenders and routed (Diod. Sic. 14.87.5–88.4).

Aeneas Tacticus

We gain a picture of broadly contemporary Greek siegecraft from a book by Aeneas 'the Tactician', who was probably the homonymous Arcadian general of the 360s BC. Aeneas tells his readers how to survive under siege, with instructions on defending walls and gates and on neutralising incendiary attacks, but the bulk of his treatise concerns guarding against treachery. In this, Aeneas simply reflects the realities of contemporary siege warfare. For example, the Spartan army operating in north-west Asia Minor in 399 BC captured a succession of towns, some by force and others by deceit (Diod. Sic. 14.38.3).

If the attacker could not rely upon betrayal from within, escalade probably remained the most common assaulting strategy. Aeneas recommends keeping assault ladders away from the walls using forked poles, and he describes an

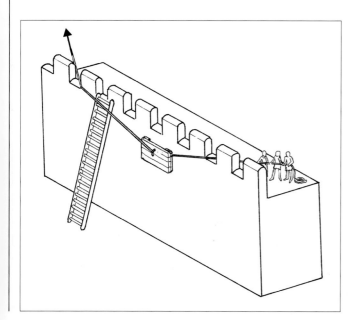

Aeneas Tacticus (36.2) describes a device for repelling assault ladders, incorporating 'a sort of door panel of planks ... with a roller underneath'. Garlan proposed the arrangement illustrated here, whereby hauling on one rope while paying out the other could sweep the ladder sideways off the wall.
(© Author, after Garlan)

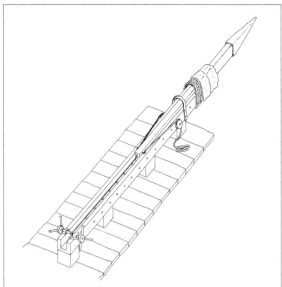

elaborate moveable framework to do the same job (36.1–2). He also appreciates that fire could be a powerful ally to both the besieger and the besieged. Besides creating a smoke screen (32.1), the defenders should use fire 'if sheds are brought up' (33.1), adding pitch, tow and sulphur to ensure a blaze. Besiegers working within missile range of the walls must have developed various types of shelters. For example, Xenophon relates how, at Egyptian Larissa in 399 BC, the Spartan general Thibron attempted to siphon off the town's water supply through a tunnel, and protected the access shaft with a wooden shed (Xen., *Hell.* 3.1.7). But the shed was burned down, a danger which Aeneas warns against for any exposed timberwork in the besieged town. He recommends fire-proofing with rawhides or a liberal coating of birdlime, a viscous substance derived from mistletoe berries, and if anything should catch fire, vinegar was the best quenching agent (33.3; 34.1).

When Aeneas mentions 'large machinery' bringing overwhelming fire-power 'from catapults and slings' (32.8), he is perhaps envisaging the kind of mobile tower used by Dionysius on Sicily. Aeneas seems to have been aware of Sicilian history – in a passage on secret messages, he alludes to events there in 357 BC (31.31) – whereas siege towers do not figure largely on the Greek mainland for another decade or so. Similarly, the catapult, by which Aeneas more probably means the *gastraphetēs* or bow-machine, must still have been rare in Greece.

As far as battering rams are concerned, Aeneas' knowledge is clearly drawn from Thucydides' description of the Peloponnesian attack on Plataea. For example, he recommends cushioning the ram's blows with sacks of chaff, bags of wool, or inflated ox-hides, and disabling the machine by lassoing the ram-head or breaking it off entirely by dropping heavy weights (32.3–6). It is true that, in 376 BC, Chabrias the Athenian besieged Naxos by 'bringing machines up to the walls and shaking the wall with them' (Diod. Sic. 15.34.4), and he seems to have used rams in his later siege of Drys (Polyaen., *Strat.* 2.22.3), but these are very much isolated incidents. Nothing similar is recorded until 350 BC, when Greek

LEFT **Aeneas (33.2) suggests that combustible material should be attached to poles, bristling with iron points 'like an engraving of a thunderbolt'. Like Philon's incendiary caltrops (*Pol.* 3.41), these could then be embedded in enemy machinery to guarantee fire damage. The standard Greek image of a thunderbolt, with spikes at both ends, is depicted on this Spartan coin. (© Hunter Coin Cabinet, University of Glasgow)**

ABOVE **At some point, the Greeks developed a variation on the battering ram, in which the beam terminated in a pointed iron head. The device, known as a *trypanon* ('borer'), is briefly mentioned by Aeneas under battering rams, and by Polyaenus in a stratagem of uncertain date. The design illustrated here is attributed to Diades, one of Alexander's engineers. (© Author, after Lendle)**

mercenaries in the service of Persia overthrew the walls of Pelusium using 'machines' (Diod. Sic. 16.49.1). We are left with the suspicion that battering rams (indeed, siege machines in general) were used only infrequently, perhaps owing to a lack of expertise, combined with the difficulties of manoeuvring heavy wheeled machinery in the mountainous Greek terrain.

Aeneas' brief section on tunnelling (37.1–9) has led to the suggestion that sieges of this period often involved the undermining of town walls. Of course, the fact that this Persian (and Carthaginian) technique must have been familiar to all readers of Herodotus does not mean that every general would have been anxious to put it into operation. Contemporary Greeks were, of course, familiar with mining technology, but, as the American scholar Josh Ober has observed, citizen soldiers would have taken a very dim view of such work, which was normally carried out by slave labour. And surely, if undermining had been at all widespread in Greek siegecraft, Aeneas would have chosen a more pertinent example than the Persian siege of Barca (37.6–7).

MACEDONIAN SIEGE WARFARE

It seems that the Greeks did not realise the full potential of mechanised siege warfare until the advent of Philip II of Macedon (r. 359–336 BC). This must be due, in part, to the fact that maintaining a siege train was expensive. But also, the possession of such equipment implied the intention to besiege repeatedly, which only arose with Macedonian imperialism. Finally, modern authorities have pointed to the willingness of Philip's full-time professional army to assault walls that would have daunted the citizen militias of the 5th century BC. More importantly, the professional character of the Macedonian army allowed for the incorporation of specialised craftsmen and engineers, without whom Alexander the Great (r. 336–323 BC) would have had no siege train.

Philip's siegecraft

Demosthenes, the great Athenian orator, railed against the Macedonian style of warfare: fighting was no longer a fair and open contest reserved for a summer's day; on the contrary, Philip might arrive outside a town at any time of year, set up his machinery, and lay siege (Dem., *Third Philippic* 50). Philip, like Dionysius before him, was particularly associated in the ancient consciousness with the development of siege machinery. Indeed, the first Greek military engineer to be mentioned by name, Polyidus the Thessalian, served 'when Philip, son of Amyntas, was besieging Byzantium' in 340 BC (Vitr., *De arch.* 10.13.3; Ath., *Mech.* 4 [10.7–10]).

De Folard's engraving depicts the snaring of a battering ram, in order to stop it working. Instead of a rope noose, as suggested by Aeneas, the crane is equipped with the grabbing device known to the Greeks as a *harpax*. (Author's collection)

Ancient writers preserve a long (but by no means exhaustive) list of Philip's conquests: Amphipolis in 357 BC, Pydna and Potidaea in 356 BC, Methone in 355 BC, Pherae and Pagasae in 352 BC, Stageira in 349 BC, Olynthus in 348 BC, Halus in 347 BC, Pandosia, Bucheta and Elataea in 342 BC (Dem., *First Olynthiac* 5, 9, 12; *Halonn.* 32; Diod. Sic. 16.52.9), not to mention the 32 Thracian towns that he razed to the ground (Dem., *Third Philippic* 26). Methone was certainly taken by assault, for it was here that Philip was struck in the eye by an arrow (Diod. Sic. 16.31.6, 34.5; cf. Polyaen., *Strat.* 4.2.15). And we know that, at Amphipolis, 'by advancing machines against the wall, and making vigorous and continuous assaults, he overthrew part of the wall with battering rams, and by entering the town through the breach, striking down many opponents, he gained possession of the town' (Diod. Sic. 16.8.2).

It is interesting that Demosthenes alleges treachery at both Amphipolis and Pydna (Dem., *First Olynthiac* 5), for the king certainly had a reputation for bribery. Mecyberna and Torone, at least, were said to have been taken 'by treachery, without the hazard of battle' (Diod. Sic. 16.53.2), and many other towns were probably taken by the same means. There was a tale that, when the inhabitants of a certain town boasted of its impregnable defences, Philip mischievously enquired whether not even gold could climb its walls (Diod. Sic. 16.54.3). And Cicero records that Philip once memorably claimed that any fortress could be taken, if only a little donkey laden with gold could make its way up to it (Cic., *Att.* 1.16.12).

However, Philip did not always enjoy success. In 340 BC, his siege of Perinthus ended in miserable failure, despite the deployment of a full siege train. Diodorus mentions 80-cubit (37m) siege towers, battering rams, and mining operations (16.74.3), and the use of arrow-firing catapults 'to destroy the men fighting from the battlements' (16.74.4). However, with Persian and Byzantine aid bolstering the Perinthian defence, Philip was soon bogged down in an impossible siege. Furthermore, his simultaneous strike on Byzantium, gambling that it had been left undefended, simply stirred up enmity among the neighbouring Greek communities, and Philip had to abandon both sieges (Diod. Sic. 16.76.4, 77.2).

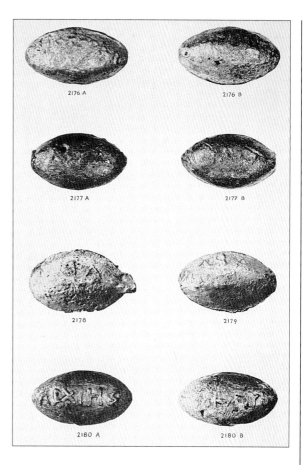

Many of the Macedonian sling bullets from Olynthus carry inscriptions. Some mention Philip or one of his generals, such as bullet 2180 (bottom row), which reads 'Archias the ready'. Others display ironic soldiers' humour, such as bullet 2176 (top row), one side of which reads 'an unpleasant gift'. (D. M. Robinson, *Excavations at Olynthus: Part X: Metal and Minor Miscellaneous Finds: An original contribution to Greek life*, plate CXXX, © 1941 The Johns Hopkins University Press. Reprinted with the permission of The Johns Hopkins University Press)

The sieges of Alexander the Great

Philip's son and successor, Alexander, had quite a different attitude to siegecraft. As Sir Frank Adcock long ago observed, 'he pressed his sieges home with fiery and resourceful determination', not with treachery and betrayal. Marsden preferred to attribute his success to the possession of superior siege machinery. It is true that, in his attack on Miletus in 334 BC, Alexander 'shook the wall with machines' (Diod. Sic. 17.22.3;

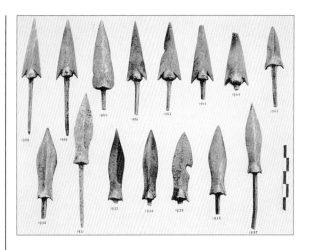

A selection of bronze arrowheads from Olynthus, many of which were probably fired by the Macedonian besiegers in 348 BC. The basic design – straight or curved sides with a solid tang for insertion into the wooden shaft – is known from Classical through to Hellenistic times. (D. M. Robinson, *Excavations at Olynthus: Part X: Metal and Minor Miscellaneous Finds: An original contribution to Greek life*, plate CXXII, © 1941 The Johns Hopkins University Press. Reprinted with the permission of The Johns Hopkins University Press)

Arrian, *Anab.* 1.19.2), creating a breach for his storming attack. And some weeks later, at Halicarnassus, his men filled the 30-cubit (13.5m) wide ditch under cover of wheeled sheds, so that machinery could be brought up (Arr., *Anab.* 1.20.8).[3] Again, Alexander 'rocked the towers and the curtain in between with rams' (Diod. Sic. 17.24.4), and the gradual destruction of the fortifications persuaded the Persian garrison to flee.

It is equally clear that Alexander was perfectly willing to launch an assault without the support of heavy machinery. For example, at Thebes in 335 BC, there was a three-day delay while he 'put together the siege machines' (Diod. Sic. 17.9.6). But, when the Thebans marched out against him, they were beaten back by the Macedonian phalanx, which proceeded to rush through the gate at their heels; the machinery was never brought into action. Similarly, the machinery assembled for attacking the main town of the Mallians in 326/5 BC did not arrive quickly enough for Alexander (Diod. Sic. 17.98.4), so he stormed the place without it. And earlier, at Sangala, he 'had his machines assembled and brought up' (Arr., *Anab.* 5.24.4), intending to batter the town wall, but by then his men had undermined it and crossed over the ruins by ladder (Curt. 9.1.18).

Of course, many factors determined whether siege machines should be used, not least the strength and situation of the defences. In 329 BC, on hearing of a revolt in Sogdiana, Alexander ordered the construction only of assault ladders; the half dozen towns affected had such low walls that they quickly fell to escalade (Arr., *Anab.* 4.2.3). But other factors might dictate whether machinery was required. During the siege of Halicarnassus, Alexander made a detour to Myndus without his siege train, expecting the town to be betrayed to him; but he was double-crossed, and although his men began undermining the walls, the arrival of a relieving force persuaded them to withdraw (Arr., *Anab.* 1.20.6).

Alexander's siegecraft is often characterised by the spectacular siege of Tyre, an island town off the coast of present-day Lebanon (see Plate D). In order to bring machinery up to the walls, the Macedonians spanned the straits with a causeway; but after spending around six months building it, Alexander must have realised that, by attacking the town on such a narrow front, he had given the advantage to the defenders. Consequently, he ordered the adaptation of ships to carry 'machines, especially battering rams' (Curt. 4.3.13; cf. Diod. Sic. 17.43.4, 46.1; Arr., *Anab.* 2.23.3), which allowed attacks to be co-ordinated all around the island. Troops were finally able to enter the town on its seaward side through breaches in the wall, while others crossed on gangways extended from the siege towers on the causeway. Although it had been a long drawn-out affair, the technical aspects of the siege impressed the ancients.

The subsequent operations at Gaza (332 BC) are more difficult to analyse, because the two surviving descriptions, by Arrian and Quintus

(continued on page 41)

3 See New Vanguard 78: *Greek and Roman Siege Machinery 399 BC–AD 363*, plate A.

THE PERSIAN SIEGE OF PALAEPAPHOS, 498 BC

THE ATHENIAN SIEGE OF SYRACUSE, 415–413 BC

DIONYSIUS' SIEGE OF MOTYA, 397 BC

ALEXANDER'S SIEGE OF TYRE, 332 BC

SCIPIO'S SIEGE OF CARTHAGO NOVA, 209 BC

PHILIP V'S SIEGE OF ECHINUS, 210 BC

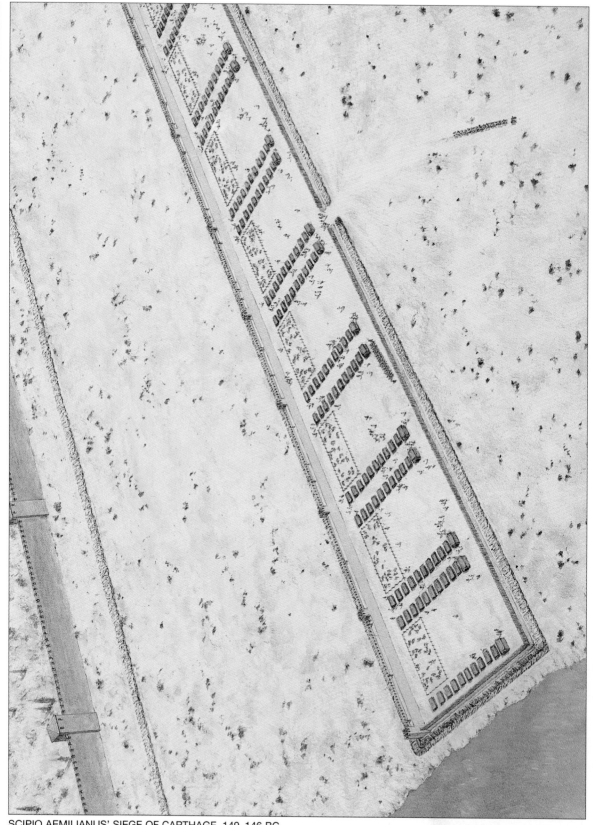

SCIPIO AEMILIANUS' SIEGE OF CARTHAGE, 149–146 BC

Curtius, are not entirely in agreement. The town's location on a high tell required a siege embankment to be piled up, which necessarily protracted the operation. Both writers mention machinery (Arr., *Anab.* 2.27.2; Curt. 4.6.9), Curtius adding the detail that the sandy ground subsided, damaging the undercarriages of the siege towers. But where Arrian concentrates on the embankment, claiming that it was 2 stades wide (370m) and 55ft high (17m), it is clear from Curtius that the main thrust of the assault involved undermining the walls (Arr., *Anab.* 2.27.4; Curt. 4.6.23).

The sieges of Tyre and Gaza highlight Alexander's ability to visualise large-scale operations, and his willingness to carry them through to completion. Similarly, at Massaga in 327 BC, there was a nine-day delay while the 'ditch of massive proportions' (Curt. 8.10.24, 30–31) was

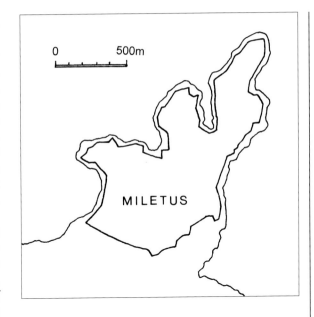

Peninsular towns were vulnerable to being 'walled off' from the mainland. Such a strategy, allegedly contemplated at Miletus both by the Athenians in 411 BC and by Alexander in 334 BC, was properly called *apoteichismos*, as distinct from the encircling *periteichismos*. (© Author)

filled; the wall was soon breached by 'machines' (Arr., *Anab.* 4.26.5), but Alexander met stiff resistance, and the townsfolk only surrendered after their chieftain was killed by a catapult arrow. More earth-moving was required at the Rock of Aornus, where Alexander's Macedonians spent seven days filling a vertiginous ravine to allow access to the impregnable stronghold (Arr., *Anab.* 4.29.7–30.1; Curt. 8.11.8–9; Diod. Sic. 17.85.6–7).

There was no place for the passive blockade in Alexander's dynamic style of siege warfare. Although we find him occasionally adopting the old Athenian strategy of *periteichismos*, or 'encirclement', this was never an end in itself. For example, during the campaign against the rebel Sogdian towns in 329 BC, Alexander instructed his general Craterus to encircle the strongest one, Cyropolis, with a ditch and palisade (Arr., *Anab.* 4.2.2). However, his intention was to contain the rebels there, while he himself recovered the other towns. Returning to Cyropolis, he

The wide isthmus that now connects the ancient island of Tyre to the mainland is thought to have resulted from centuries of silting around the remains of the Macedonian causeway. (© IFAPO)

began a battering attack and, while the defenders were fully occupied, infiltrated the town along a dry watercourse, repeating a stratagem used by the Persians at Babylon, 300 years before. The gates were thrown open from within and, after a fierce struggle, the town was captured.

Macedonian siege machines

Philip's place in the development of siege warfare is secure, but Marsden was intrigued by his failure at Perinthus. He suggested that, around 350 BC, Philip established permanent workshops for mechanical engineering, but that inadequacies were shown up during the campaign of 340 BC, and a new chief engineer had to be appointed for the siege of Byzantium. This was the context into which Marsden placed Polyidus, whose service he dated to the years 340–335 BC. Of course, this is all conjectural. Polyidus' name was certainly linked with the building of a giant siege tower (*helepolis*) at Byzantium (*Lat. Alex.* 8.5–7), but we cannot say whether this event stood at the beginning of his career or at the end.

Marsden's scheme perhaps gains support from the fact that Polyidus' pupils, Diades and Charias, 'campaigned with Alexander' (Vitr., *De arch.* 10.13.3; Ath., *Mech.* 4 [10.9–10]), probably from the very start. They were perhaps responsible for developing the wheeled shed or 'tortoise' (*chelone*, or *testudo*), which thereafter became increasingly common in siegecraft, particularly for carrying battering rams up to the wall. In antiquity, Diades became famous as 'the man who captured Tyre with Alexander' (*Lat. Alex.* 8.12–15), and it was perhaps during that siege that he developed his famous boarding bridges; later writers lamented the fact that his instructions for assembling these were never written down (Vitr., *De arch.* 10.13.8; Ath., *Mech.* 9 [15.5–7]).

The massive and complex machinery often deployed by Macedonian armies must have been expensive to manufacture. Faced with failure at Pherae, Philip was determined to withdraw his machinery intact, so he set his engineers the task of dismantling it by night. Such an operation left his men vulnerable to counter-attack, so they made it sound as if they were constructing new machines; the terrified townsfolk spent the night strengthening their defences, and were in no position to contest Philip's surreptitious departure (Polyaen., *Strat.* 4.2.20). Such large machines were also troublesome to transport. After the fall of Miletus, Alexander had his siege train carried to Halicarnassus by sea (Diod. Sic. 17.24.1), and the artillery used at Gaza was shipped from Tyre (Arr., *Anab.* 2.27.3). Transfer by land must have been more difficult, but we know that Diades designed his siege towers to be disassembled (Vitr., *De arch.* 10.13.3), and it was presumably this innovation that permitted Alexander to use machinery in the mountainous terrain of the Hindu Kush.

Macedonian artillery

Marsden believed that Alexander's frequent deployment of artillery was made possible by the technical advances of his father's engineers. As a hypothesis, this has much to commend it, not least the fact that contemporary Athenian comedy represented Philip as surrounded by catapults (Mnes., *Philip* frg. 7), and a word-list composed around AD 180 contains an entry for *katapeltai Makedonikoi* ('Macedonian catapults'),

The explorer Sir Aurel Stein identified the site of Aornus with Pir-sar, the flat-topped ridge to the left of the photograph. Alexander approached from the west (right) where the 150m-deep Burimar-kandao ravine had to be bridged by a timber-framed embankment. (J. F. C. Fuller, *The Generalship of Alexander the Great*, Eyre & Spottiswoode, London, 1958, plate 4)

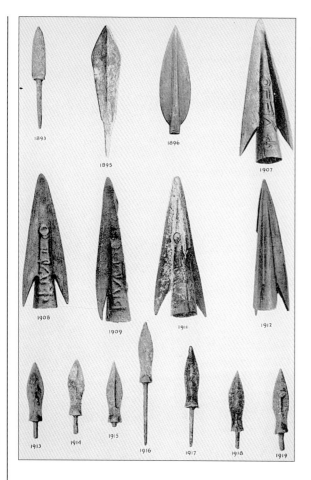

suggesting some special relationship with Macedon. The development of the torsion catapult must have been a slow process of trial and error, and the stone-projectors that first appear at Halicarnassus and Tyre cannot have been particularly powerful. Diodorus must be exaggerating when he says that, at Tyre, Alexander 'struck down the walls with stone-projectors, and with arrow-firers forced back the men standing on the battlements' (Diod. Sic. 17.42.7). The use of arrow-firers in this suppressing role is expected, but it is extremely doubtful whether stone-projectors could ever have demolished masonry walls.

Some towns of the eastern Mediterranean were already equipped with catapults. Byzantium loaned some to Perinthus in 340 BC, Halicarnassus had them in 334 BC, and the Tyrians had 'a great abundance of catapults and the other machines needed for sieges' (Diod. Sic. 17.41.3). Even the Persian troops who halted Alexander at the Persian Gates appear to have been equipped with catapults; besides rolling gigantic boulders down from the heights on either side of the pass, Arrian alleges that they fired volleys of arrows from 'machines' (Arr., *Anab.* 3.18.3). In Marsden's opinion, these catapults were of the *gastraphetēs* variety, but the question must remain open; even if torsion technology was funded by Macedon, as seems likely, peripatetic engineers could still have spread it around the eastern Mediterranean.

A selection of bronze arrowheads from Olynthus. The top three (1893/5/6) may be 5th century Persian, but the others are probably Macedonian. The large triple-barbed examples (approximately 7cm long) are inscribed with Philip's name; Marsden suggested that they might have been fired from a large *gastraphetēs*-type catapult. (D. M. Robinson, *Excavations at Olynthus: Part X: Metal and Minor Miscellaneous Finds: An original contribution to Greek life*, plate CXX, © 1941 The Johns Hopkins University Press. Reprinted with the permission of The Johns Hopkins University Press)

HELLENISTIC SIEGE WARFARE

The so-called *Diadochoi*, or successors of Alexander, are better known for their field battles, and it is commonly assumed that little emphasis was placed on siege. Of course, where one side sought refuge behind walls, the other had no recourse but to employ whatever besieging skills were available to them. Directly after Alexander's death, an Athenian army under Leosthenes defeated the Macedonian regent, Antipater, and shut him up in the town of Lamia in central Greece. When assaults on the walls proved fruitless, Leosthenes resorted to a blockading strategy and began surrounding the place with a wall and ditch (Diod. Sic. 18.13.3); only his accidental death in a mêlée around the siege-works brought an end to the operation.

In the winter of 317/16 BC, Antipater's son Cassander similarly surrounded Pydna with a stockade running from sea to sea, intending to assault the walls when better weather arrived. But, in the meantime, the garrison suffered so badly from famine that cavalry horses were slaughtered for food and the townsfolk allegedly resorted to cannibalism (Diod. Sic. 19.49.1–50.1). Much the same strategy had been adopted by

Antigonus, the commander in Asia Minor, when he cornered Eumenes in the Armenian fortress of Nora (320 BC). Diodorus records how he surrounded the place with 'double walls and ditches and astonishing palisades' (Diod. Sic. 18.41.6) and continued the blockade for a year. (It was during his captivity that Eumenes evolved a novel method of exercising his cavalry horses using a machine, so that they would remain fit for battle.)

Not every general was so ready to embrace passive siegecraft. When Perdiccas, who had fallen heir to Alexander's grand army, invaded the Egyptian kingdom of Ptolemy, his first objective was the so-called Camel Fort; but, although he combined an escalade with the unusual tactic of assaulting the palisade with elephants, he could not dislodge Ptolemy's troops and was forced to withdraw (Diod. Sic. 18.34.1–5). A different type of assault was tried by Arridaeus against the offshore town of Cyzicus, with 'all sorts of missiles, and both arrow-firing and stone-projecting catapults, and all the other supplies fit for a siege' (Diod. Sic. 18.51.1); but without naval support his attack failed. Elephants again formed the centrepiece in the attack on Megalopolis by Polyperchon, when he succeeded Antipater as regent of Macedon in 319 BC. Although the townsfolk had repaired their fortifications and constructed new arrow-firing catapults, Polyperchon's forces managed to undermine a long stretch of wall, under covering fire from siege towers. The elephants were then directed into the breach, but when they trod on the spiked doors that the Megalopolitans had laid in their path they ran amok, maddened by pain, and created havoc among Polyperchon's troops (Diod. Sic. 18.71.3–6).

Demetrius Poliorcetes

Consolidating his hold on Asia Minor and the Middle East, Antigonus was able to take Joppa and Gaza by storm. But the 15 months he spent reducing Tyre to capitulation (Diod. Sic. 19.61.5) stand in stark contrast to Alexander's dynamic siege of the same town, a generation earlier. By contrast, Antigonus' son Demetrius, known to posterity as Poliorcetes, 'the besieger', is commonly credited with raising siegecraft to the pitch of perfection. Certainly, one of his closest advisors, named Philip, may well have been Alexander's engineer of the same name. And it is true that Demetrius enjoyed a string of successes, for example in 307 BC, when he captured Piraeus, Munychia, Megara, Ourania and Carpasia. In the following year, he captured Salamis on Cyprus despite the fact that the townsfolk managed to destroy his siege train in the process. But it is curious that he is chiefly remembered for his siege of Rhodes in 305/4 BC, which was a signal failure. As the Greek scholar Arnold Gomme long ago observed, Demetrius was not *ekpoliorketēs*, 'taker of cities', but simply 'besieger of cities'; the nickname seems to have been applied in derision after his failure at Rhodes.

Later generations clearly misconstrued the insult; Diodorus, for one, believed it was due to his 'devising many things beyond the skill of the engineers' (20.92.2). On the contrary, Demetrius' siege tactics show no particular innovations, but he is rightly remembered for the scale of his siege machinery. He is thought to have been the sponsor of the enormous ram-carrying tortoise designed by Hegetor of Byzantium; and the giant siege tower, or *helepolis* ('city-taker'), became something of a

The citadel at Corinth, known as the Acrocorinth, viewed from the north. When Demetrius assaulted the town in 303 BC, the garrison of the citadel was intimidated into surrender by his military reputation. (© Author)

hallmark, although the largest one ever built, at Rhodes, failed to overawe the defenders.[4]

Several ancient accounts of the siege of Rhodes relate how Demetrius was repeatedly repulsed, and even had to withdraw the *helepolis* when it was set ablaze by the Rhodians; finally, Antigonus advised his son to make peace with the town. Vitruvius alone records the colourful story that a Rhodian engineer named Diognetus foiled the *helepolis* by pumping water, mud and sewage into its path; the huge machine, he says, 'settled in the quagmire that had been created, unable afterwards to either advance or retreat' (Vitr., *De arch.* 10.16.7).

Early Rome

While the new developments in machinery and artillery were being explored in the eastern Mediterranean and on Sicily, quite a different style of siege warfare was being practised in Italy. Our main source for early Roman history is Livy, supplemented to some extent by Dionysius of Halicarnassus; both writers were active in Augustan Rome (*c.*25 BC), long after many of the events they describe, and scholars generally doubt the accuracy of their narrative prior to around 300 BC. For example, both authors describe the siege of Corioli in 493 BC, renowned as the event from which the young Coriolanus took his name. According to Livy, the besieging army was caught between a Volscian relief column and a sortie from within the town, but Coriolanus led a daring charge through the open gates and set fire to the place (Livy

---

4 See New Vanguard 78: *Greek and Roman Siege Machinery 399 BC–AD 363*, plate C for the *helepolis*; plate D for Hegetor's tortoise.

2.33); this is substantially the story later preserved by Plutarch (*Coriolanus* 8). Dionysius, on the other hand, incorporates battering rams, wicker screens and ladders into his account (6.92.1–6), although it is generally acknowledged that this kind of equipment was unknown in 5th (or even 4th) century BC Roman warfare; consequently, Dionysius has been accused of exaggeration, if not complete fabrication.

The most famous of the early Roman sieges was undoubtedly the reduction of the Etruscan town of Veii in 396 BC; the operations allegedly stretched over ten years, but the parallel with the legendary siege of Troy has raised suspicions. Here again, events are tied up with a celebrated hero: in this case, the upright Marcus Furius Camillus, who famously punished a Falerian schoolmaster for offering to betray his town to the Romans. It is likely that, as with Corioli, a kernel of truth was gradually embellished to glorify the central character. Early in the siege, prior to Camillus' arrival, the Romans are supposed to have tried 'towers, shelters, sheds and the other apparatus for besieging a city' (Livy 5.5), to no avail; but these elements were probably a later addition, designed to make Camillus' subsequent success seem all the more impressive. Equally unlikely is the tale that Camillus sent picked troops to tunnel up into the rocky citadel and open the gates from within. Interestingly, the locality is known for its honeycomb of drainage tunnels, which perhaps gave rise to this popular story.

It must be remembered that Rome in the late 4th century was a city-state struggling to dominate its neighbours in the Italian peninsula. It was entirely oblivious to events on nearby Sicily, where Syracuse was again locked in combat with Carthage, and the tyrant Agathocles was employing the full range of besieging tactics, from encirclement and undermining at Croton (295 BC) to the use of machinery at Utica (307 BC); the siege tower at the latter even had enemy prisoners nailed to the sides in a gruesome attempt at psychological warfare (Diod. Sic. 20.54.2–7). By contrast, Roman sieges of the period were relatively unsophisticated affairs. Livy records the storming of Murgantia, Ferentinum and Romulea in 296 BC, the latter at least by escalade (Livy 10.17), and in 293 BC the gates of Aquilonia were broken open by troops who were formed up into the *testudo* formation with shields locked over their heads (Livy 10.41).

Fortifications

Unsettled conditions in the Greek world of the later 4th and 3rd centuries BC prompted a renewed interest in town fortifications. The precise dating of these is notoriously difficult. For example, it has been said that the recessed gateway, standing inside an open courtyard flanked by towers, was a response to the development of mechanised siegecraft. This layout is certainly found in the late 3rd century circuits of Perge and Side, but it was already used at Messene, where it ought to date from the foundation of the town in 369 BC (Diod. Sic. 15.66.1). It is often suggested that the plentiful provision of minor, so-called postern gates indicates a dating in the later 4th century. This was a time, it is argued, when infantry adopted a vigorous strategy of 'aggressive defence', counter-attacking siege machinery outside the walls; however, the gates could equally be intended to cater for the peacetime activities of the local population.

Another diagnostic feature favoured by scholars is the tower. Larger, taller varieties are often taken to imply the presence of defensive

The late Eric Marsden with his reconstruction of a three-span arrow-firer at Maiden Castle (England). This machine, designed to shoot arrows 69cm long, was probably the standard catapult from the 3rd century BC until the 1st. (P. Johnstone, *Buried Treasure*, Phoenix House, London, 1957, plate 61)

artillery, particularly where windows (rather than archers' loop-holes) are evident. However, the study of towers is a complex one, and the existence of a large floor area does not automatically imply that a large catapult was to be accommodated. In general, towers fulfilled a range of functions, which included sheltering sentries and enabling archers to enfilade adjacent stretches of curtain wall, not forgetting the equally important role of surveillance.

When catapults became available for town defence in the later 4th century BC, they were surely stationed under cover, for protection from sun, rain and enemy action; furthermore, the need for a clear operating space, to allow the machine and its crew to work quickly and effectively, would most easily have been met in a tower chamber. However, the Carthaginian defence of Lilybaeum against Pyrrhus in 274 BC demonstrates that, in time of need, catapults could easily be deployed along the walls (Diod. Sic. 22.10.7). Marsden believed that it was crucial to gain an advantage in range by placing catapults as high as possible, but no ancient writer ever expresses this opinion. In fact, the behaviour of torsion artillery rather encourages the opposite belief, that the accuracy of short-range targeting and the direct impact of a low trajectory were preferred.[5]

SIEGE WARFARE DURING THE ROMAN REPUBLIC

The Greek writer Polybius compiled a history of the Roman world from 264 to 146 BC; as a military man, he gives a fairly reliable picture of siege warfare during these years. The First Punic War (264–241 BC), which

5 See New Vanguard 89: *Greek and Roman Artillery 399 BC–AD 363*, p. 21.

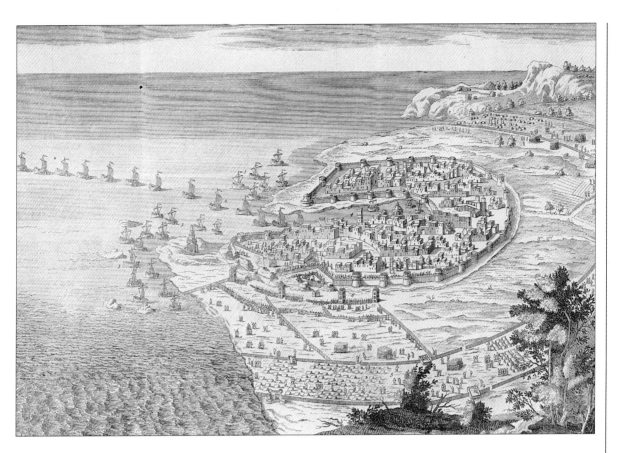

took Roman troops overseas for the first time, involved a handful of sieges on Sicily, where many of the towns were still held by Carthaginian garrisons. But the Romans lacked the equipment and expertise to besiege effectively, and the war was decided in naval encounters.

The siege of Agrigentum (the Greek Akragas) in 262 BC provides a case in point. The Romans surrounded the town with double ditches, the inner guarding against sorties from the town, the outer against a relieving force, in an effort to starve the garrison into submission (Polyb. 1.18.2–3). But after five months of static blockade, the besiegers themselves were running short of provisions and suffering from dysentery, and although they easily defeated a Carthaginian relief column their negligence permitted the garrison to escape from the town by night. In the following year, a seven-month blockade of Mytistratum failed (Diod. Sic. 23.9.3), and the town was only taken three years later, when the townsfolk willingly opened their gates to the Romans (Zonaras 8.11). Most tellingly, at Lilybaeum, down the coast from the old Carthaginian base at Motya, the Roman siege dragged on for ten years without resolution. Initially adopting an assaulting strategy, the Romans managed to demolish a length of fortifications using machinery perhaps supplied by their ally Hiero, the tyrant of Syracuse; but they were repulsed by vigorous Carthaginian counter-attacks (Polyb. 1.42.8–13; 45.1–14). The siege soon degenerated into stalemate, largely because the Romans failed to seal the town's harbour, which left the blockade incomplete; when the war ended in 241 BC, the town still had not fallen.

At Lilybaeum, Polybius records that the Romans built two camps and linked them with a ditch, a palisade and a wall. De Folard's imaginative reconstruction shows the town surrounded by double earthworks, as at Agrigentum, while Carthaginian ships continue to ply in and out of the harbour unmolested. (Author's collection)

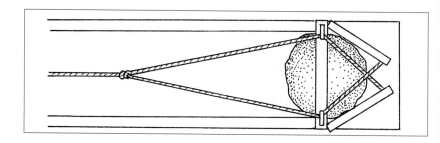

Philon of Byzantium

Siege warfare of the period is illuminated by the work of Philon, who wrote a *Mechanical Encyclopedia* (*Mēchanikē Syntaxis*) in the later 3rd century BC. Besides a section on constructing artillery (*Belopoiika*), the encyclopedia included instructions for both the besieged and the besieger; modern editors usually run these together to form a single book on siegecraft (*Poliorkētika*).

In general, it is clear that Philon expected the attacker to use wheeled machinery. For example, he suggests the use of tunnels to draw away any material with which the attacker has filled the town's defensive ditch (*Pol*. 1.36); the filling of ditches always preceded the advance of machinery.[6] In addition, he suggests burying large storage jars outside the defences, upright and with their mouths stopped up with seaweed and concealed by a layer of soil, to trap the wheels of enemy sheds and machinery (*Pol*. 1.76).

He is especially concerned about stone-projecting catapults. It is unlikely that these were ever powerful enough to demolish a wall, but they could wreak havoc along the battlements. Philon says that the merlons ('the topmost blocks of stone', in his words) should be fastened down so that the stone-projector's missiles would glance off and not demolish them (*Pol*. 1.8). He also recommends that the battlements should be padded with palm-wood boards and nets filled with seaweed (*Pol*. 3.3–5), and that window shutters should be iron-plated inside and outside, so that stone-projectors could not shatter them (*Pol*. 1.23).

When he turns to besieging, Philon mentions encirclement almost as an afterthought, and only in connection with a blockade: '[a town can be taken] by starvation, surrounding it with a palisade and fortifying a strong position against the town, and garrisoning it with steadfast guards to prevent anyone bringing in [supplies] by land or by sea' (*Pol*. 4.84). By contrast, almost his first recommendation for capturing a town is to 'secretly approach the wall by night with ladders, in wintry weather or when the townsfolk are drunk at some public festival, and capture some of the towers' (*Pol*. 4.4). The Achaean capture of the Acrocorinth in 243 BC, for example, was achieved by scaling an unusually low section of the defences (Plut., *Aratus* 18.4; 21.2–3). To counter just such an eventuality, Philon recommends building walls at least 20 cubits (9m) high 'so that ladders brought up against them will not reach' (*Pol*. 1.12). And in a frequently misunderstood passage, he reiterates that 'it is necessary, regarding those towers which will face attack by machinery, to build them high and strong, but the others [i.e., where machinery cannot approach] only so that ladders will not reach' (*Pol*. 1.26). Later, he lists various counter-measures for hindering and dislodging ladders, by using

6 See New Vanguard 78: *Greek and Roman Siege Machinery 399 BC–AD 363*, pp. 13–15 and plate A.

beams 'bent like an anchor', forked poles, and caltrops (*Pol.* 1.79), and by throwing fire from above (*Pol.* 3.39). These are much the same methods recommended by Aeneas Tacticus over a century earlier, and they remained common throughout the period.

Hannibal and Carthaginian siegecraft

Hannibal sparked off a new war with Rome in 219 BC when he attacked Saguntum in Spain. The methods he employed hark back to the Carthaginian sieges on Sicily in the 400s BC. First, battering rams were brought forward under the protection of shelters, and the wall was breached. Then, when the townsfolk repulsed the Carthaginian assault and hastily repaired the damaged wall, Hannibal resorted to undermining, with covering fire from artillery in a siege tower. Battering rams were simultaneously reapplied elsewhere around the town perimeter, but the town's strong fortifications and hilltop location enabled it to hold out for eight months (Livy 21.15.3). Appian, a writer who flourished in the AD 140s but who clearly used earlier sources of information, says that Hannibal had the place surrounded by a closely guarded ditch (App., *Hisp.* 10); although this sounds like a *periteichismos*, it is clear that Hannibal intended no passive blockade. In fact, combining the old technique of encirclement with an active assaulting strategy was not entirely novel, as Antigonus had done something similar at Caunus in 313 BC (Diod. Sic. 19.75.5).

But it was in the use of machinery that Hannibal's siegecraft differed from contemporary Roman efforts. Livy records how, at Nola in 216 BC, the Carthaginians had 'all the equipment for besieging a town' (Livy 23.16.11), and they only resorted to blockading Petelia because the townsfolk persisted in burning their machines. Among the equipment that Hannibal brought up to the walls of Cumae, pride of place went to an immense wheeled tower, but it too was destroyed by fire (Livy 23.37.2–4). Finally, Appian lists Hannibal's equipment at Tarentum as 'towers and catapults and sheds and hooks' (App., *Hann.* 33).

The operations at Tarentum spanned 213–209 BC. Its initial betrayal to Hannibal by disaffected townsfolk forced the Roman garrison to take refuge in the citadel, which lay on a promontory between the sea and the harbour. The garrison were in no danger of starvation, as they were easily supplied (and even reinforced) by sea, but the Carthaginians hemmed them in with a palisade, a ditch and rampart, and a wall (Livy 25.11.7). As at Saguntum, Hannibal clearly intended to assault the position with various kinds of siege equipment; but, when the Romans sallied out and burned it, a stalemate ensued (Polyb. 8.32.3–34.2). In 209 BC, betrayal again delivered the town, this time to the Romans. Hannibal's Italian mercenaries guarding a particular sector of wall were persuaded to turn a blind eye to the Roman escalade, and the assault was co-ordinated with a break-out from the besieged citadel. Caught in between, the Tarentines were subjected to looting and indiscriminate slaughter.

Roman siegecraft in the Second Punic War

In 218 BC, Cnaeus Scipio, uncle of the famous Scipio Africanus, employed blockade against the Carthaginians' allies in Spain: at Atanagrum, his army 'sat down around the town' (Livy 21.61.6), forcing surrender within days, and the same treatment brought the Ausetani to heel after only 30 days. There is no mention of siege-works on those occasions, and Roman armies operating in Greece in the 190s BC sometimes used cordons of troops to cut off and intimidate enemy towns. However, when three Roman armies converged on pro-Carthaginian Capua in 212 BC, they elected to blockade the town with an encirclement, known to the Romans as a 'circumvallation'. Nothing similar had been attempted by a Roman army since Agrigentum, 50 years earlier. There, the town had been encircled by two lines of ditches. Here, according to Appian, 'they dug a ditch around Capua and in addition to the ditch they built a wall in a circle round the whole place. Then the generals built another one outside the encircling wall, using the middle as a camp. There were battlements turned towards the besieged Capuans, and others towards those outside, and the appearance was of a great city with a smaller one in the middle' (App., *Hann.* 37).

The choice of strategy perhaps depended as much upon the commanding officer's temperament as upon the available resources and the lie of the land. In 214 BC, Claudius Marcellus and Fabius Maximus, nicknamed *Cunctator* ('the delayer'), met stiff resistance at Carthaginian-occupied Casilinum. Fabius' instincts were to withdraw, but Marcellus brought up 'shelters and all the other sorts of works and machinery' (Livy 24.19.8); at the sight of this, the townsfolk panicked and fled, and the garrison was captured. However, Roman armies of the day were generally ill-equipped for full-blown mechanised operations. Only during the siege of Utica, up the coast from Carthage, do we hear of machinery on any significant scale. Here, in 204 BC, Scipio requisitioned artillery and machines from Sicily, where it is likely to have been captured from the

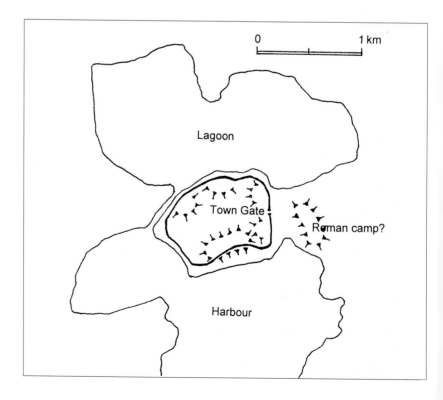

The ancient town of Carthago Nova (modern Cartagena, Spain) was situated on a peninsula; the narrow neck of land to the east provided the only access. However, while the defenders were distracted by an all-out assault on the town gate, they failed to notice a Roman escalading party wading across the unexpectedly shallow lagoon to the north of the town. (© Author)

Carthaginians, and set up field workshops to manufacture more. Although the siege ultimately failed, Appian claims that Scipio raised siege embankments in order to bring his battering rams into play (App., *Pun.* 16).

If this is true, it represents a breakthrough in Roman siegecraft. Until then, most sieges were conducted as straightforward storming operations, for example at the Italian town of Arpi, where a heavy downpour drowned the noise of the assault and kept the guards under cover, where they could not interfere (Front., *Strat.* 3.9.2). In 209 BC, Scipio Africanus' capture of heavily fortified Carthago Nova was achieved by an audacious assault (see Plate E), and three years later, at Ilourgia, he threatened to scale the wall himself, in order to embolden his troops, who were despondent after their initial failure. Ladder length was always critical to the success of an escalade. Plutarch claims that Marcellus himself studied the Epipolae wall at Syracuse to ensure that his ladders would reach (Plut., *Marc.* 18.3), a precaution that Scipio perhaps omitted at Carthago Nova, where many of the ladders were too short (Livy 26.45.2). For the siege of Locri in 205 BC, the Romans persuaded some craftsmen to assist them by letting down ladders over the wall (Livy 29.6–8); local knowledge presumably ensured that they were long enough.

The state of Roman siegecraft in the late 3rd century is encapsulated by the events at Syracuse, which was targeted by Marcellus in 213 BC after it switched allegiance to Carthage. He advocated a two-pronged assault, co-ordinating his naval attack on the Achradina sea wall with his colleague Claudius Pulcher's land attack on the Epipolae plateau from the north. However, he had reckoned without the genius of Archimedes, the renowned Syracusan mathematician. Plutarch claims that Archimedes was disdainful of practical mechanics (Plut., *Marc.* 17.3-4); but he rose to the challenge of defending his native town, chiefly with catapults of various sizes to ensure complete coverage of all the approaches, but also with machines that capsized the Roman ships.[7] The Romans soon resorted to blockading the town, but early in 212 BC, in the midst of celebrations in the town, Marcellus managed to seize the Epipolae plateau in a nocturnal escalade (Front., *Strat.* 3.3.2) which followed the precepts of Philon to the letter (above, p. 50). Although the garrison of the formidable Euryalus fortress soon surrendered, the Achradina fell only after another lengthy blockade. It is said that one of the victims of the final looting, late in 212 BC, was Archimedes; unwilling to leave his current mathematical calculation incomplete, he was killed resisting his Roman captors (Livy 25.31.9).

Carthage itself came under siege in 149 BC in the so-called Third Punic War, when it refused to

Having cut Carthage off from its hinterland with siege-works, Scipio Aemilianus proceeded to seal the harbour entrance, completing his blockade. His troops then broke into the city from the captured quayside. (© Author)

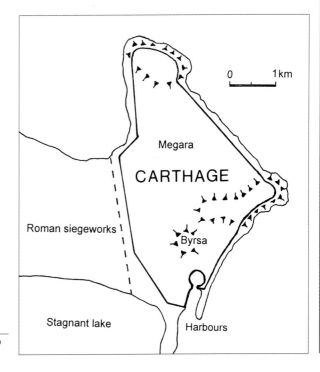

CARTHAGE

Megara

Roman siegeworks

Byrsa

Stagnant lake

Harbours

0   1km

7 See New Vanguard 78: *Greek and Roman Siege Machinery 399 BC–AD 363*, p.33.

comply with Rome's ruthless demands for the city to be destroyed. Having already surrendered and dutifully disarmed, handing over 2,000 catapults in the process, it began desperately re-arming; hundreds of weapons were manufactured each day and, as an emergency measure, newly built catapults were allegedly sprung with women's hair (App., *Pun.* 93). Initial Roman assaults proved incompetent, until Scipio Aemilianus arrived late in 147 BC. He blockaded the city on the landward side with a linear version of the Capuan circumvallation (see Plate G), and by concentrating his efforts on the harbour he finally broke into the Byrsa citadel and captured the city.

Rome and Macedon

In the late 3rd and early 2nd centuries BC, Roman armies campaigned in Greece, against Macedon, Sparta and the Aetolian League. Artillery was often present, courtesy of Rome's alliance with Pergamon and Rhodes, and machinery became more frequently employed, but sieges remained firmly based on the storming assault. At the same time, there was something of a revival in Macedonian siegecraft under Philip V (r. 221–179 BC) and his son Perseus (r. 179–168 BC), and Macedon's brief alliance with Rome (192–189 BC) perhaps led to some cross-fertilisation of ideas.

The Macedonians were always ready to employ undermining tactics, despite the inherent dangers. In 217 BC, the army of Philip V spent nine days tunnelling towards the town of Phthiotic Thebes, and another three days undermining its walls for a distance of 60m, but the mine collapsed prematurely, and perhaps buried the sappers beneath the ruined wall (Polyb. 5.100.2–5). Similar operations at Palus in the previous year had gone without a hitch: the wall was undermined and propped with wood, the town was invited to surrender, and when it refused the props were fired and the wall collapsed; but Philip's treacherous lieutenant Leontius deliberately botched the final assault (Polyb. 5.4.6–13). At Prinassus in 201 BC, and at Lamia ten years later, the bedrock proved too hard for tunnelling. At the latter, Philip's opportunistic co-operation with Rome backfired when his allies ordered him to desist, and he was forced to leave empty-handed (Livy 36.25.1–2). But at the former, he deceived the townsfolk by a cunning ruse: the Macedonians made the noise of mining by day and heaped up soil brought from elsewhere by night, so that, when Philip claimed to have underpinned 60m of wall, the Prinassians were convinced and surrendered their town (Polyb. 16.11.2–6). The stratagem was so ingenious that it later featured in the works of both Frontinus (*Strat.* 3.8.1) and Polyaenus (*Strat.* 4.18.1).

Philip rarely built his strategy around machinery, perhaps owing to the difficulty of transporting such cumbersome devices around the Greek landscape. A full siege train can be glimpsed only once, at Echinus (see Plate F), a town easily approached by sea. Similarly, although Philip clearly had access to artillery, it was used sparingly. More often, he relied on the storming assault, for example at Psophis (219 BC), where three divisions of ladder-carrying troops made simultaneous assaults on the walls; the town was captured when the garrison, charging out through a postern, was repulsed and chased back through the open gate (Polyb. 4.70–72).

Contemporary Roman armies continued to use similar methods. In 200 BC, Claudius Cento mounted a dawn raid on the major Macedonian base at Chalcis. Some troops with ladders seized a tower and the adjacent sector of wall, before quietly making their way to the gates and breaking them open to admit the entire army; in the ensuing chaos, a fire broke out, destroying an arsenal full of artillery (Livy 31.23.1–24.3). But ladders were not the only means to scale a wall. Heracleum was captured in 169 BC by troops who clambered up the walls by standing on top of a *testudo* shield formation (Livy 44.9.1–10).

Machinery was gradually introduced wherever necessary. At Atrax in 198 BC, Quinctius Flamininus threw up a siege embankment to carry rams up to the wall, and although his troops entered the town through the resulting breach they were repulsed by the Macedonian garrison. The siege tower that Flamininus then deployed almost fell over when one of its wheels sank in the rutted embankment, and the Romans finally gave up (Livy 32.18.3). Their failure can probably be attributed to inexperience in mechanised siege warfare: first, their siege embankment was obviously insufficiently compacted to bear the weight of heavy machinery; and second, they seem rarely to have used a siege tower before. Polybius mentions towers among the equipment destroyed at Lilybaeum 50 years earlier (Polyb. 1.48.2), but these may well have been supplied by Hiero and were hardly a resounding success in any case.

At Heraclea in 191 BC, Acilius Glabrio divided his forces into four squads and set them a competition to build siege equipment; in a few

The fortifications at Cnidus (Turkey) defend a large area surrounding two harbours, and climb the hills to the acropolis (top right). Philip V attacked the town unsuccessfully in 201 BC. (A. W. McNicoll, *Hellenistic Fortifications from the Aegean to the Euphrates*, Oxford University Press, Oxford, 1997, plate 25. Reprinted by permission of Oxford University Press and Ms T. Winikoff)

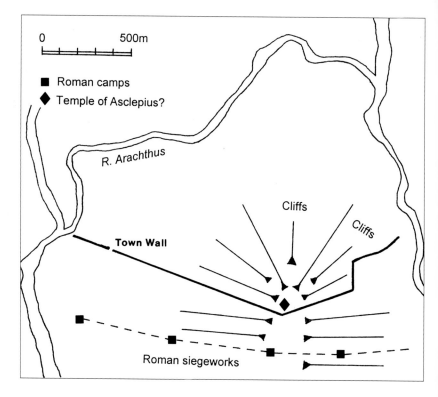

The late Professor N. G. L. Hammond's topographic study forms the basis of this reconstruction of the Roman siege of Ambracia in 189 BC. Livy mentions camps linked by an earthwork facing the citadel, but none of this survives on the ground. (© Author)

0   500m

■ Roman camps
◆ Temple of Asclepius?

R. Arachthus

Cliffs

Cliffs

Town Wall

Roman siegeworks

days, they had erected embankments and constructed siege towers, battering rams and shelters, but the town finally fell to a dawn escalade. Even at Ambracia, which Fulvius Nobilior invested in 189 BC, the Romans pressed the siege actively, although they had hemmed the town in with a siege wall. The defenders employed a full range of countermeasures, including dropping heavy weights on the Roman battering rams and using grappling irons to seize Roman siege weapons; wall breaches were quickly repaired; and raids were mounted by day and night to burn Nobilior's machinery. When the Romans resorted to tunnelling, the townsfolk foiled their attempt by filling the tunnel with noxious smoke.

Ambracia only surrendered when the siege reached deadlock. However, smaller towns frequently surrendered, not as a last resort, but immediately, from fear of a Roman storming attack. They wished to avoid the fate of towns like Antipatrea: in 200 BC, the Roman general Lucius Apustius 'attacked and took the place by storm, killed all the men of military age, gave all the booty to his troops, demolished the walls, and burned down the town' (Livy 31.27.4). In 199 BC, Celetrum initially refused a Roman request to capitulate, but promptly surrendered at the sight of a *testudo* formation of troops approaching its gates (Livy 31.40.1–3). Similarly, the Roman fleet had scarcely disembarked its siege equipment on the island of Andros, when the islanders abandoned their defences and fled (Livy 31.45.3–8). Gytheum held out a little longer, when under attack in 195 BC, but having seen their walls collapse to a combination of undermining and battering, the townsfolk rapidly surrendered (Livy 34.29.5–13). And in 190 BC, although the Phocaeans put up a spirited defence, they realised they were doomed without the assistance of their Syrian allies, so they surrendered.

EPILOGUE

From Cyrus to Scipio

If the Persians and Carthaginians were notorious for their merciless treatment of captured towns, the Romans often matched their excesses. In 146 BC, when the Romans crushed the Achaean League, Corinth was laid waste by the Roman general Lucius Mummius (Paus. 2.1.2). The Greeks, already defeated in battle, did not attempt to hold the city, and the Romans entered through the open gates; they slaughtered any men who remained, auctioned off the women, children and slaves, and carried off everything of value (Paus. 7.16.5). By extraordinary coincidence, the same year saw Scipio's final destruction of Carthage. As the Romans entered the city, they became embroiled in street fighting; whole areas of multi-storey housing were set ablaze, with their inhabitants still in residence, and any who survived were unceremoniously despatched by the troops clearing the streets. Appian says that, for six days and nights, the soldiers were rotated, 'so as not to be distressed from want of sleep, hard labour, slaughter, and unpleasant sights' (App., *Pun.* 129–130).

The brutal treatment of Carthago Nova in 209 BC was allegedly typical of Roman armies, with the slaughter of inhabitants, even including dogs and other animals, and the looting of the town by

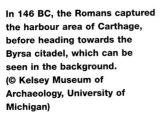

In 146 BC, the Romans captured the harbour area of Carthage, before heading towards the Byrsa citadel, which can be seen in the background. (© Kelsey Museum of Archaeology, University of Michigan)

designated troops, while others stood guard (Polyb. 10.15.4–9). But different generals clearly managed their siege operations in different ways. At the surrender of Gytheum, the undisciplined Roman troops commenced wholesale looting, despite the orders of their general Aemilius Regillus, who asserted that towns which surrendered ought not to be plundered; although he failed to exert his authority, he managed to protect any townsfolk who gathered in the forum (Livy 37.32.1–14). It was presumably to retain some measure of control that Marcellus, during the penultimate phase of the siege of Syracuse, decreed that there should be no bloodshed, only looting (Livy 25.25.5), but in the final sack he was obliged to set guards at any locations he did not want despoiled, such as the royal treasury.

After Cyrus' looting of Babylon in 539 BC, he is portrayed assuring his troops that 'it is a custom amongst all peoples at all times that, whenever a town is conquered in war, the people in the town and their goods belong to the captors' (Xen., *Cyr.* 7.5.73). This was as much the philosophy of Scipio as of Cyrus. And in Classical Greece, plunder belonged, first and foremost, to the general. He seems usually to have reserved the lion's share for the state treasury, after subtracting expenses and awarding prizes to deserving combatants; as a contribution towards defraying the costs of war, the proceeds might be used to provide soldiers' pay. A well-known pronouncement by Philip V shows him closely controlling the goods plundered by his army, in much the same way that contemporary Roman generals did: officers were entrusted with receiving the plunder for equitable division, at the general's discretion (Polyb. 10.16.2–9). Thus, at Carthage, Scipio Aemilianus rewarded the troops, while reserving the bullion and the contents of the temples. The general could even forgo his own entitlement, as Mummius is said to have done, when he distributed the spoils of Corinth throughout Italy (Front., *Strat.* 4.3.15). Nevertheless, the decision rested with the conquering general, following a precedent set 400 years earlier by Cyrus at Sardis (Hdt. 1.89).

FURTHER READING

There are few general works on ancient siege warfare. Paul Bentley Kern's *Ancient Siege Warfare* (Souvenir Press, London, 1999) concentrates on the treatment of captured cities from earliest times down to AD 70. Peter Connolly's *Greece and Rome at War* (Greenhill Books, London, 2nd edn, 1998) has an appendix on 'Fortifications and siege warfare', discussing a handful of well-known Greek and Roman examples with good illustrations. The fundamental study of Greek siegecraft is Yvon Garlan's *Recherches de poliorcétique grecque* (Boccard, Paris, 1974), although it covers only the 5th and 4th centuries BC; there is no comparable study of later centuries.

English translations of the main historical sources are available in the Loeb Classical Library. For Aeneas Tacticus, there is also a translation and commentary by D. Whitehead (*Aineias the Tactician. How to survive under siege*, Clarendon Press, Oxford, 1990), and much of Philon's *Poliorkētika* has been translated by A. W. Lawrence (*Greek Aims in Fortification*, Clarendon Press, Oxford, 1979).

SELECT BIBLIOGRAPHY

Adcock, F. E., *The Greek and Macedonian Art of War*, University of California Press, Berkeley, 1957

Briant, P., 'A propos du boulet de Phocée', in *Revue des Études Anciennes* 96 (1994), 111–114

Erdmann, E., *Nordosttor und Persische Belagerungsrampe in Alt-Paphos. I. Waffen und Kleinfunde*, Universitätsverlag, Konstanz, 1977

Greenewalt, C. H., Jr., 'When a mighty empire was destroyed: the common man at the fall of Sardis, ca. 546 BC', in *Proceedings of the American Philosophical Society* 136 (1992), 247–71

Grundy, G. B., *Thucydides and the History of his Age*, J Murray, London, 1911

Maier, F. G., 'Ausgrabungen in Alt-Paphos: Stadtmauer und Belagerungswerke', in *Archäologischer Anzeiger* 1967, 303–30

–, 'Ausgrabungen in Alt-Paphos. Sechster vorläufiger Bericht', in *Archäologischer Anzeiger* 1974, 28–48

Marsden, E. W., *Greek and Roman Artillery. Historical Development*, Clarendon Press, Oxford, 1969

–, 'Macedonian military machinery and its designers under Philip and Alexander', in *Ancient Macedonia* 2 (1977), 211–223

Ober, J., 'Hoplites and obstacles', in V. D. Hanson (ed.), *Hoplites. The Classical Greek Battle Experience*, Routledge, London, 1991, 173–196

Özyiğit, Ö., 'The city walls of Phokaia', in *Revue des Études Anciennes* 96 (1994), 77–109

Pritchett, W. K., *The Greek State at War*, Part 5, University of California Press, Berkeley, 1991

Winter, F., *Greek Fortifications*, Routledge, London, 1971

Relief sculpture from the Nereid Monument (Block 878). On the left, the towered wall of a citadel can be seen, occupied by soldiers, one of whom raises his hand to throw a stone. The scene to the right is thought to depict besiegers requesting the defenders' capitulation. Behind the horse, there may be traces of a siege embankment carrying soldiers over the wall.
(© The British Museum)

THE PLATES

A: THE PERSIAN SIEGE OF PALAEPAPHOS, 498 BC

No description of the siege exists, but the archaeological remains give a good indication of the course of events. The Persian strategy was based on the construction of an earthen embankment, which the defenders sought to counter by digging tunnels underneath. The excavator believed that the embankment was designed to bring a siege tower against the town wall. No depiction of Persian machinery survives, but a device resembling the ancient Assyrian battering ram may be thought plausible.

The large quantities of arrowheads, spearheads and stone missiles from the area in front of the battlements suggest bitter fighting, and the two Greek-style helmets found in the debris of the embankment indicate that the Persians may have deployed a unit of Greek mercenaries.

B: THE ATHENIAN SIEGE OF SYRACUSE, 415–413 BC

The scene is from 414 BC. Having established a fort at Syca ('the fig tree') on the Epipolae plateau above Syracuse, the Athenians embarked upon their usual strategy of encirclement (*periteichismos*). Specialist masons and carpenters appear to have accompanied the army to Sicily, and tools for construction work were a normal part of their equipment.

For their siege-works, Athenian besieging armies used whatever materials were to hand. Thucydides indicates that, at Syracuse, some of the Athenians were divided into work gangs or guard details, while others were assigned the task of collecting stone and timber, which they laid out at intervals across the plateau. It was some of these materials that the Syracusans appropriated to construct their counter wall. It is likely that the Athenian siege-works were of dry stone construction with a wall-walk protected by timber battlements.

C: DIONYSIUS' SIEGE OF MOTYA, 397 BC

Dionysius probably utilised the existing causeway as a track for his siege machines, and concentrated his assault on the north gateway. This theory gains some support from the fact that the roadway here was strewn with arrowheads and covered with mud-brick debris, apparently from collapsed fortifications.

Dionysius' machinery included six-storey wheeled towers. No ancient author describes how such contraptions were moved, but it seems likely that brute force was used, with relays of labourers pushing against any available surface. Besides carrying the drawbridges that were needed for a storming assault, the towers also afforded an elevated firing platform for missile troops. This siege represents the first historical mention of the catapult, which at this early date probably means the *gastraphetēs*, or 'belly bow'.

D: ALEXANDER'S SIEGE OF TYRE, 332 BC

Alexander allegedly mobilised tens of thousands to construct the causeway, 2 *plethra* (62m) wide and 4 stades (740m) long. Building materials came from the demolition of the old town on the mainland, and timber was brought from the mountains of Lebanon; entire trees and rocks were heaved in to build up the structure. Wicker screens protected the workmen, and

The 18th-century *Chevalier* de Folard made a study of ancient military science, accompanied by detailed engravings. This one shows how the fire chamber at the end of a siege mine was intended to work. The tunnels at Palaepaphos were on a much smaller scale.
(Author's collection)

two siege towers were erected so that missile troops could provide covering fire. The Tyrians responded with a fire-ship, a large transport vessel filled with combustible material and guided under sail against the causeway; cauldrons slung from the yardarms were rigged to set the boat ablaze when it reached its goal. In the event, considerable damage was done, including the destruction of the siege towers, but Alexander's engineers set to work again and the causeway was finally completed.

Nothing now remains of the town fortifications, but Arrian's claim that the walls were 150ft (46m) high is absurd. Both Diodorus and Curtius indicate that the walls were well furnished with arrow-firing catapults, and the city engineers had contrived all sorts of devices to counter the

Soldiers man the battlements in this scene from the Heroon at Trysa, where the seated couple perhaps represent the town's ruling elite. Outside the walls, more soldiers shelter beneath their shields, while others infiltrate the town through an open postern.
(© Kunsthistorisches Museum, Vienna)

Relief sculpture from the Heroon at Trysa, thought to date from around 370 BC. Three soldiers assault the walls under cover of their shields, while the townsfolk adopt the age-old defence of dropping boulders onto them, and hurling stones and spears.
(© Kunsthistorisches Museum, Vienna)

Macedonians. There were screens of stretched hides to protect the defenders, and a variation, padded with seaweed, was later lowered over the battlements to absorb the impact of flying stones. Also illustrated is an example of the 'iron hand' or *harpax*, used to grab individual men or machines.

E: SCIPIO'S SIEGE OF CARTHAGO NOVA, 209 BC

The Carthaginian foundation of Carthago Nova (New Carthage) lay in a lagoon, with only one avenue of approach, from the east. When the Romans arrived outside the town, the garrison, bolstered by the townsfolk, rushed out to join battle, but were driven back within their walls. Scipio (later named Africanus for his victory at Zama in 202 BC) immediately launched an escalade, but many of the ladders were too short to be useful, and the Romans made no progress in the face of a staunch defence.

A renewed attempt was co-ordinated with the sending of a *testudo* formation against the gates; protected by a roof of shields, the Romans hacked the timber gates with swords and axes. A simultaneous assault on the north wall went unnoticed, and the Romans were able to open the gates from within and seize the town.

F: PHILIP V'S SIEGE OF ECHINUS, 210 BC

Polybius gives a full description of the siege-works erected by Philip V of Macedon outside the town of Echinus. There was a battlemented gallery running parallel to the town defences, with a great wheeled ram shed positioned at either end, so that the siege-works themselves resembled a section of town wall; rearward communications were secured by the provision of covered passages. Three heavy catapults were deployed, comprising a one-talent stone-projector (i.e., a catapult designed to shoot stones weighing approximately 26kg) flanked by half-talent machines (i.e., designed for stones weighing approximately 13kg). In addition, Philip began driving two tunnels towards the town, with the intention of undermining the walls.

Little now remains of the town, but we have suggested a standard battlemented wall with two-storey towers sited roughly a bowshot apart to give mutual support. It is unlikely that a minor town like Echinus could have afforded catapults, and its defence would have been based on archery fire and thrown projectiles. Philip's assault was never carried through because the town surrendered when its Roman allies failed to dislodge the Macedonian besiegers.

G: SCIPIO AEMILIANUS' SIEGE OF CARTHAGE, 149–146 BC

The scene shows the state of play in 147 BC, when Scipio Aemilianus arrived to take over the management of the siege. As previous assaults had failed, Scipio decided to impose a blockade. Appian describes the elaborate siege-works, which consisted of a pair of fortifications stretching across the 4½km isthmus, one facing inwards, the other facing outwards. The two were linked at each end, to form a long, thin encampment. Three of the sides were palisaded, while the fourth side, facing Carthage, was actually a 12ft (3.7m) wall with battlements and towers. Construction was completed in 20 days. It is possible that the interior was laid out like a regular temporary camp, with the repeating pattern of tent-lines to accommodate the legionary maniples (units of around 160 men) and their officers. Nothing has survived of the city wall of Carthage, which was allegedly a 15m-high mud-brick barrier, fronted by a ditch, 5m wide.

OPPOSITE **The excavation of the south gate at Motya in 1962. (B. S. J. Isserlin & J. du Plat Taylor,** *Motya. A Phoenician and Carthaginian City in Sicily*, **Brill, Leiden, 1974, plate 13. Reprinted with the permission of B. S. J. Isserlin)**

OPPOSITE BELOW **View over the harbour area of Carthage, taken in 1925. The Bay of Tunis can be seen in the background. (© Kelsey Museum of Archaeology, University of Michigan)**

De Folard's engraving depicts the disabling of a battering ram using a stratagem employed by the Plataeans. First, they suspended a large beam by chains fastened to the ends of two poles which projected horizontally from the top of the wall; then, having drawn the beam upwards, the chains were suddenly slackened, so that the beam crashed down onto the enemy machine. (Author's collection)

INDEX